I Love it Coloring Books
Today you will be Inspired

I0468154

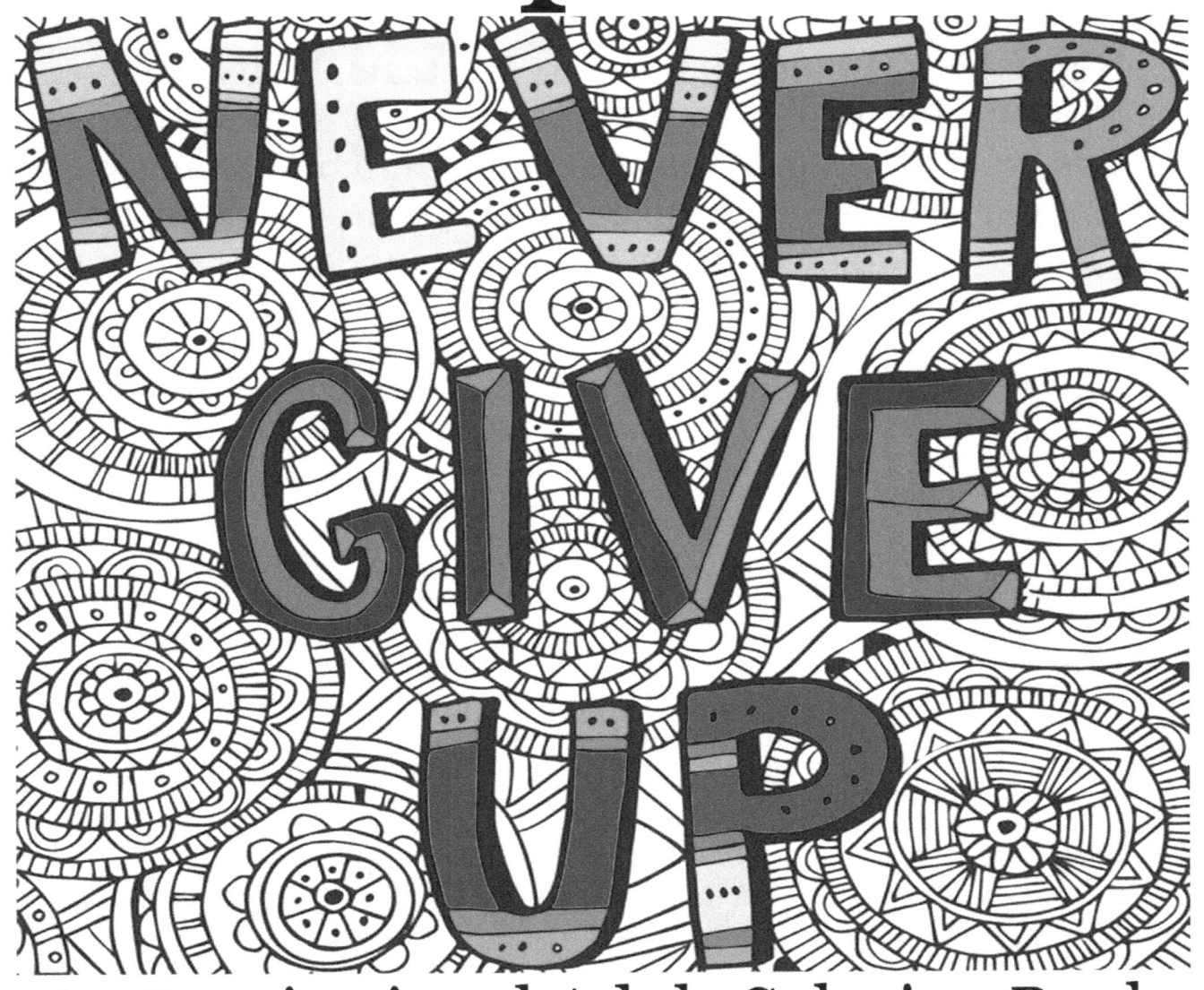

An Inspirational Adult Coloring Book
Featuring 33 Stress Relieving Inpirational Quotes

Clara Hughes

Featuring 33 inspirational quotes to help brighten your day these designs range in complexity from beginner to intermediate and provide hours and hours of stress relief, mindful calm, and fun, creative expression.

Clara Hughes lives in Florida with her four cats, Fluffy, Tab, bunny and pepper. She loves to draw, and with a quirky sense of humor, her designs are not only cute but often quite humorous. Claras ink drawings are the perfect choice for young and old alike and are suitable for pencil, crayon, marker or water colors.

I Love it Coloring Books - Today you will be inspired - An Inspirational Adult Coloring Book
By: Clara Hughes - I love it Coloring Books
Copyright I love it coloring books

ISBN-13: 978-1530927609

ISBN-10: 1530927609

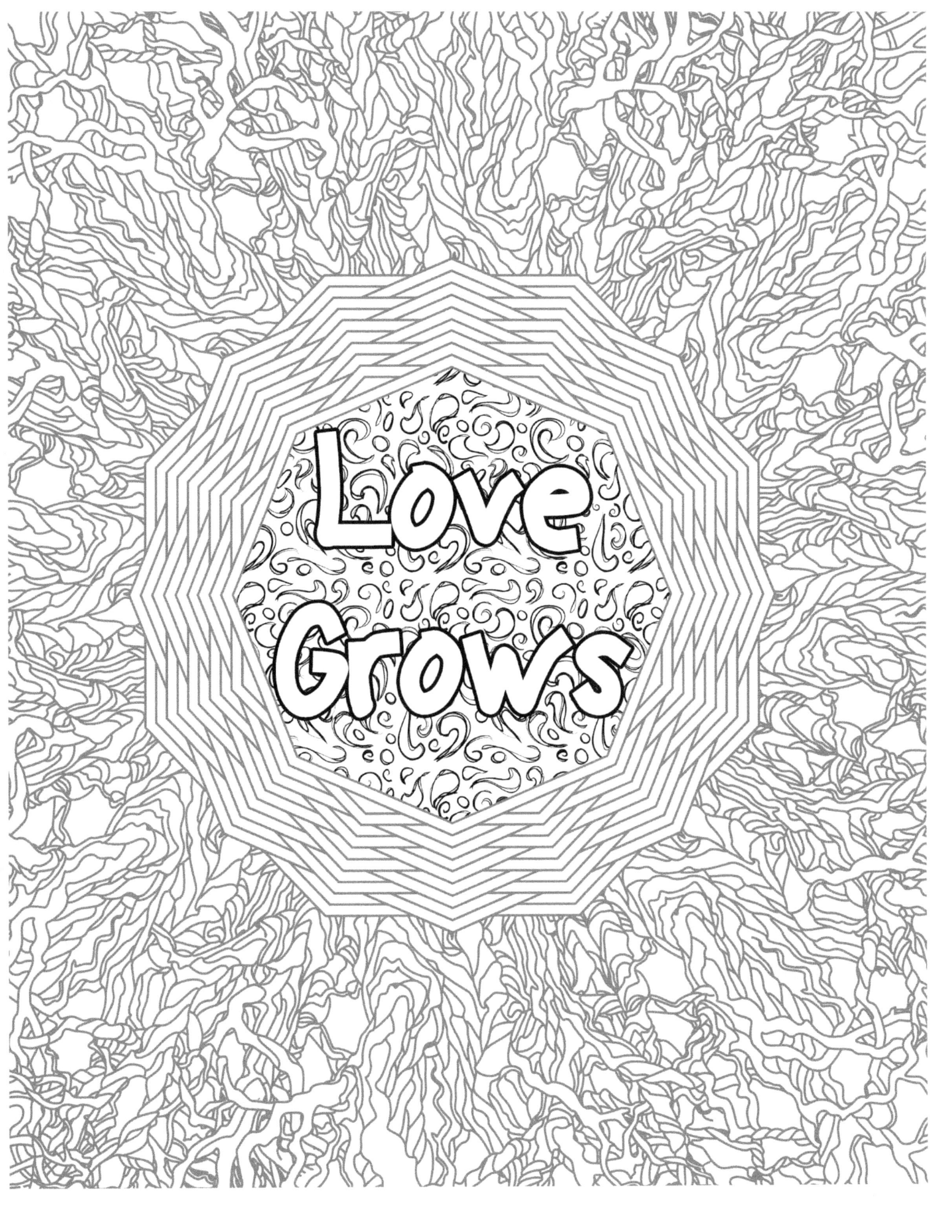

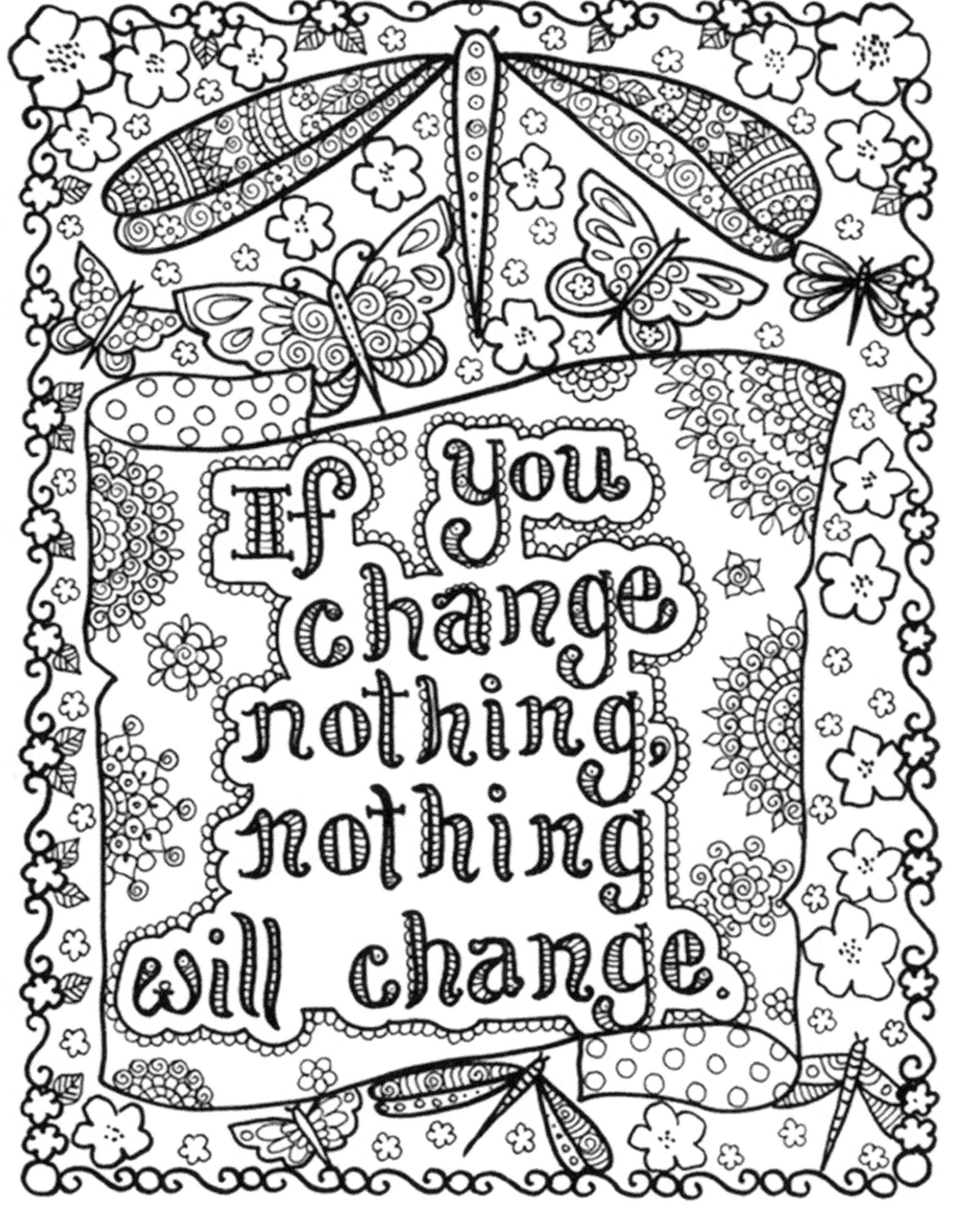

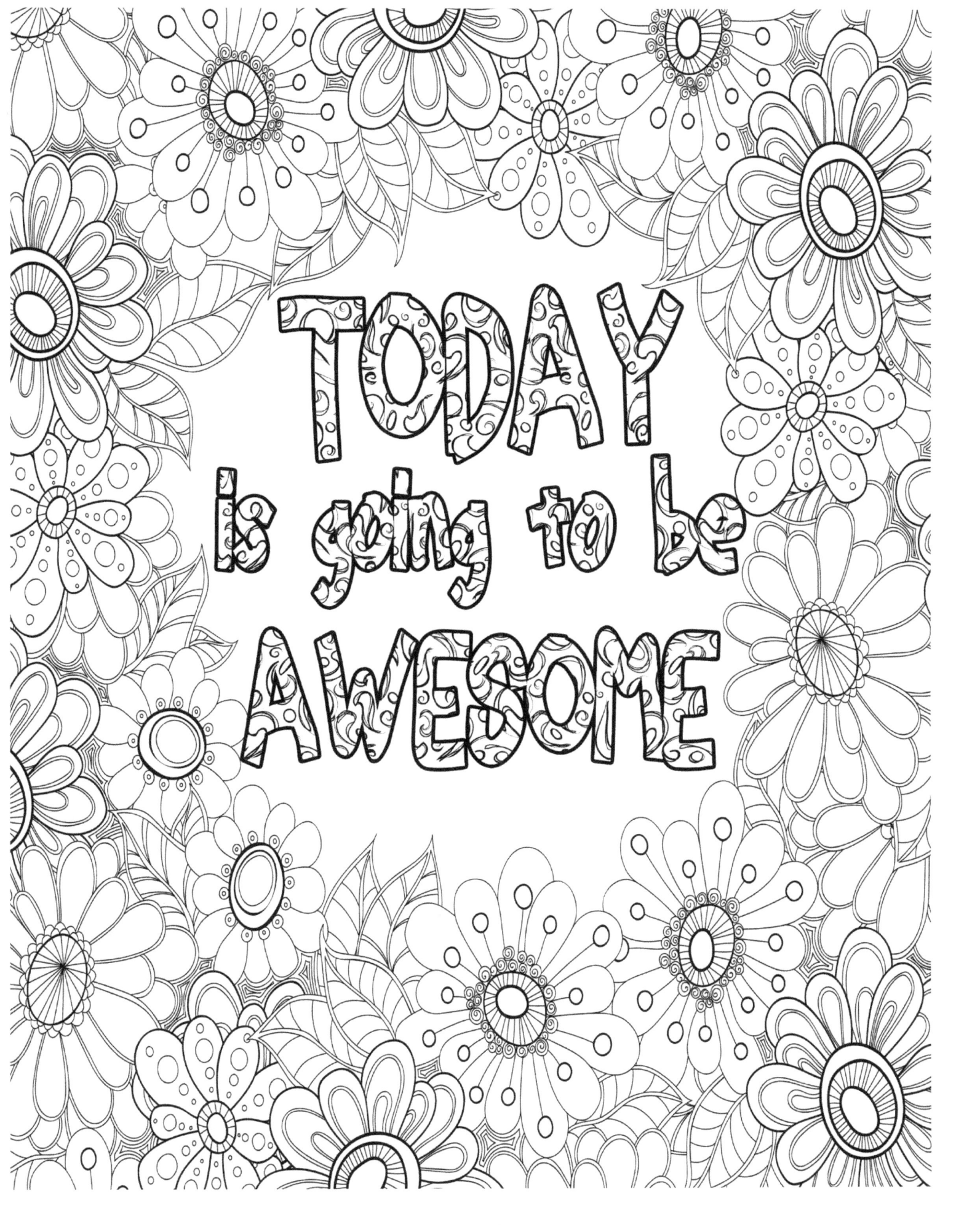

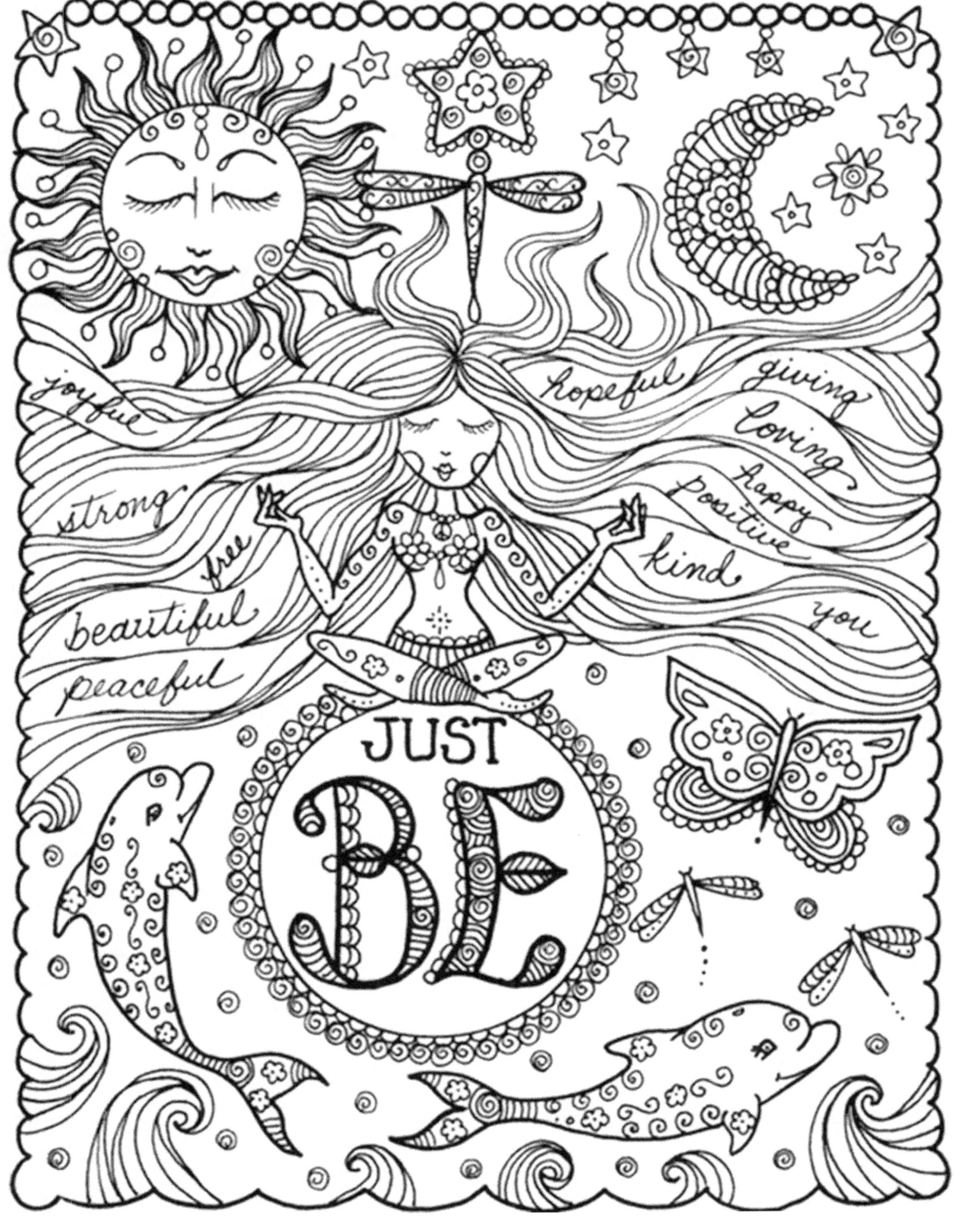

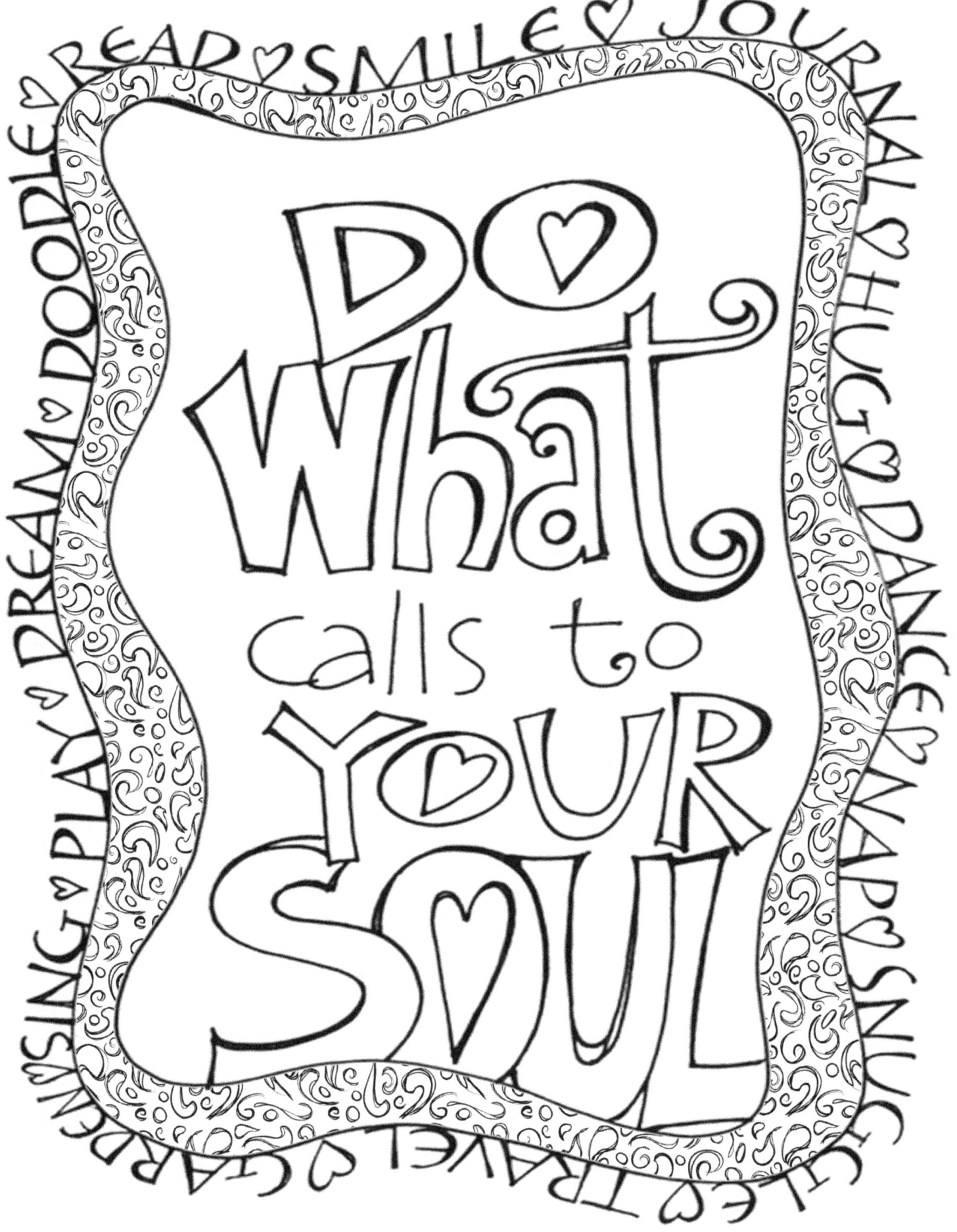

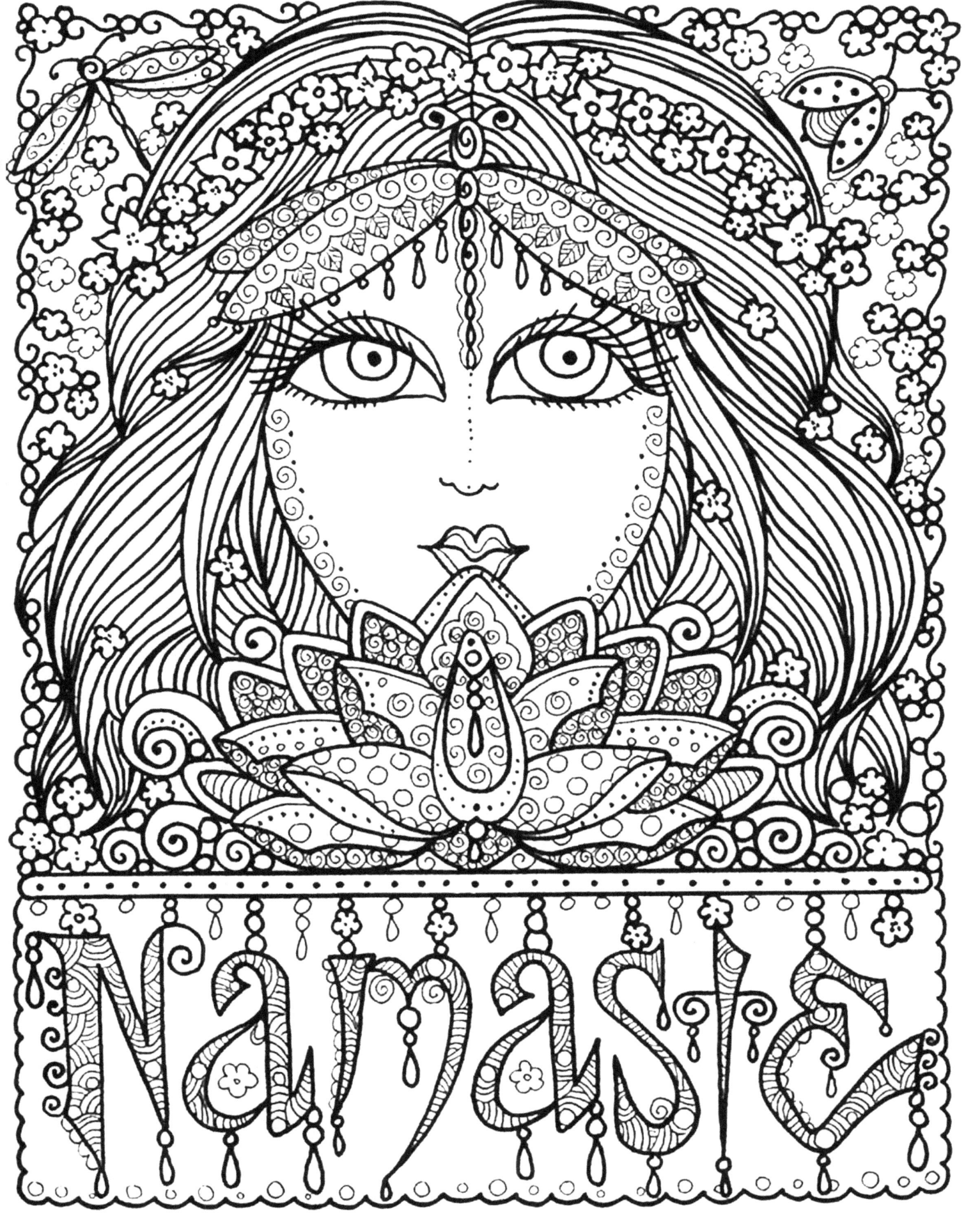

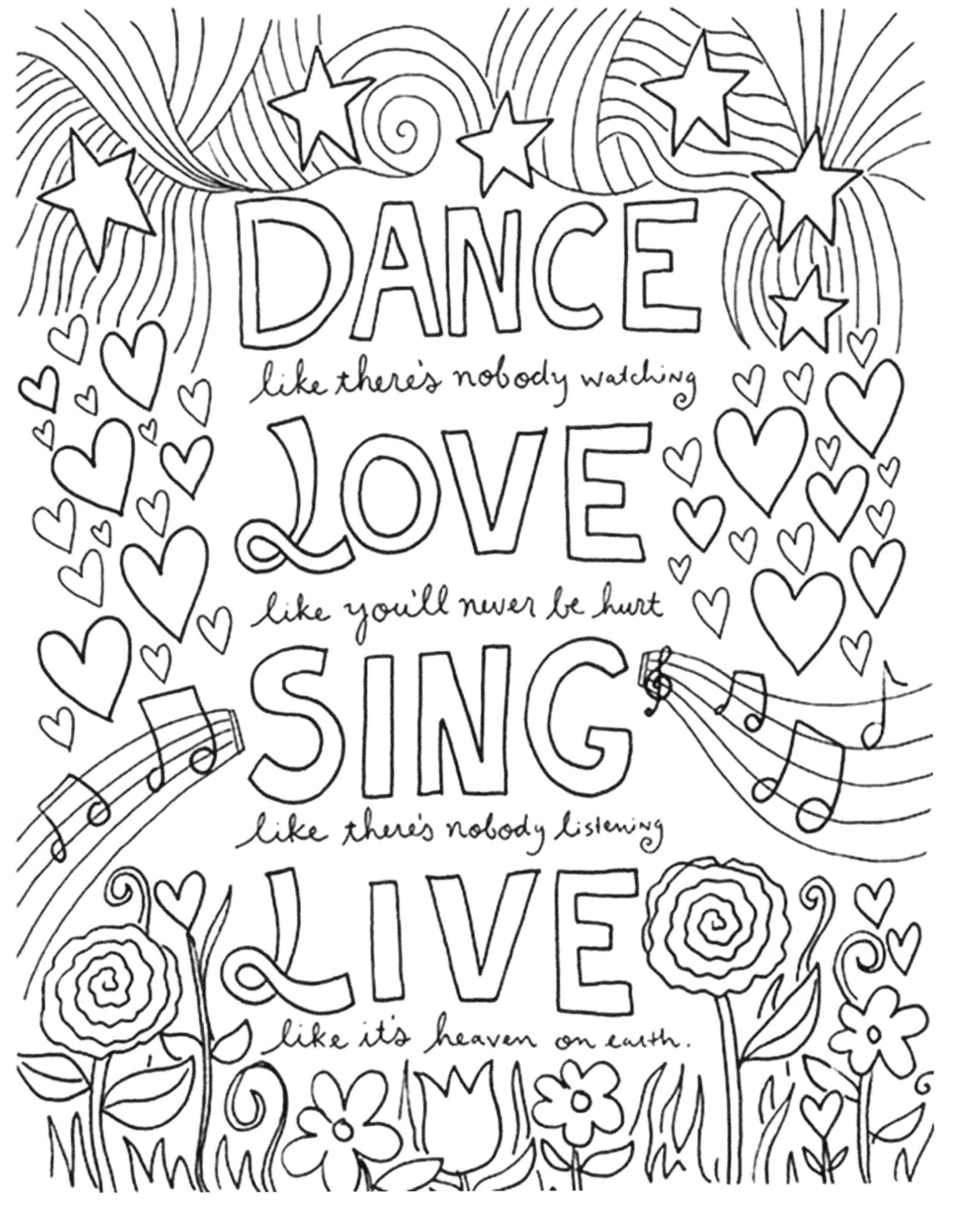

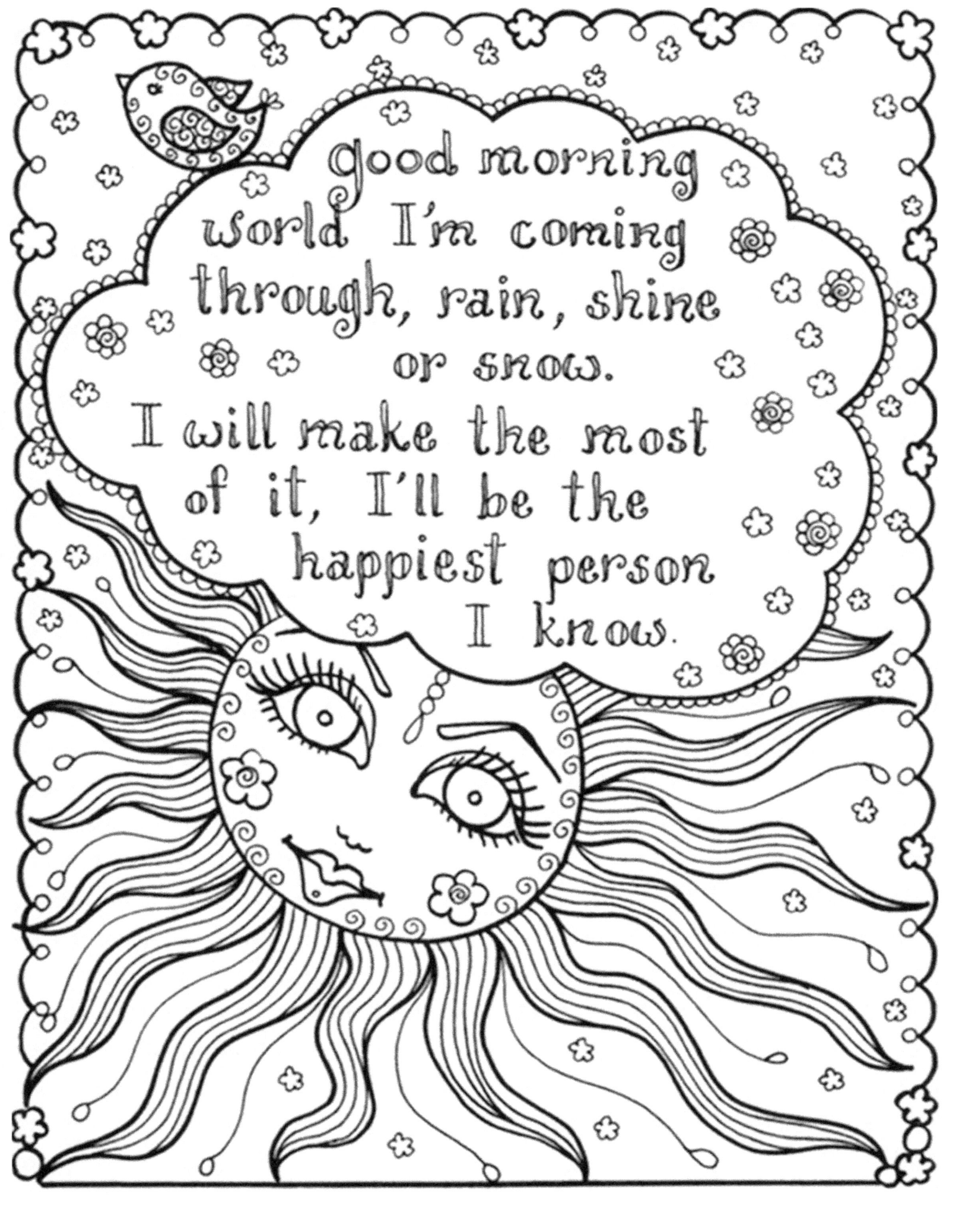

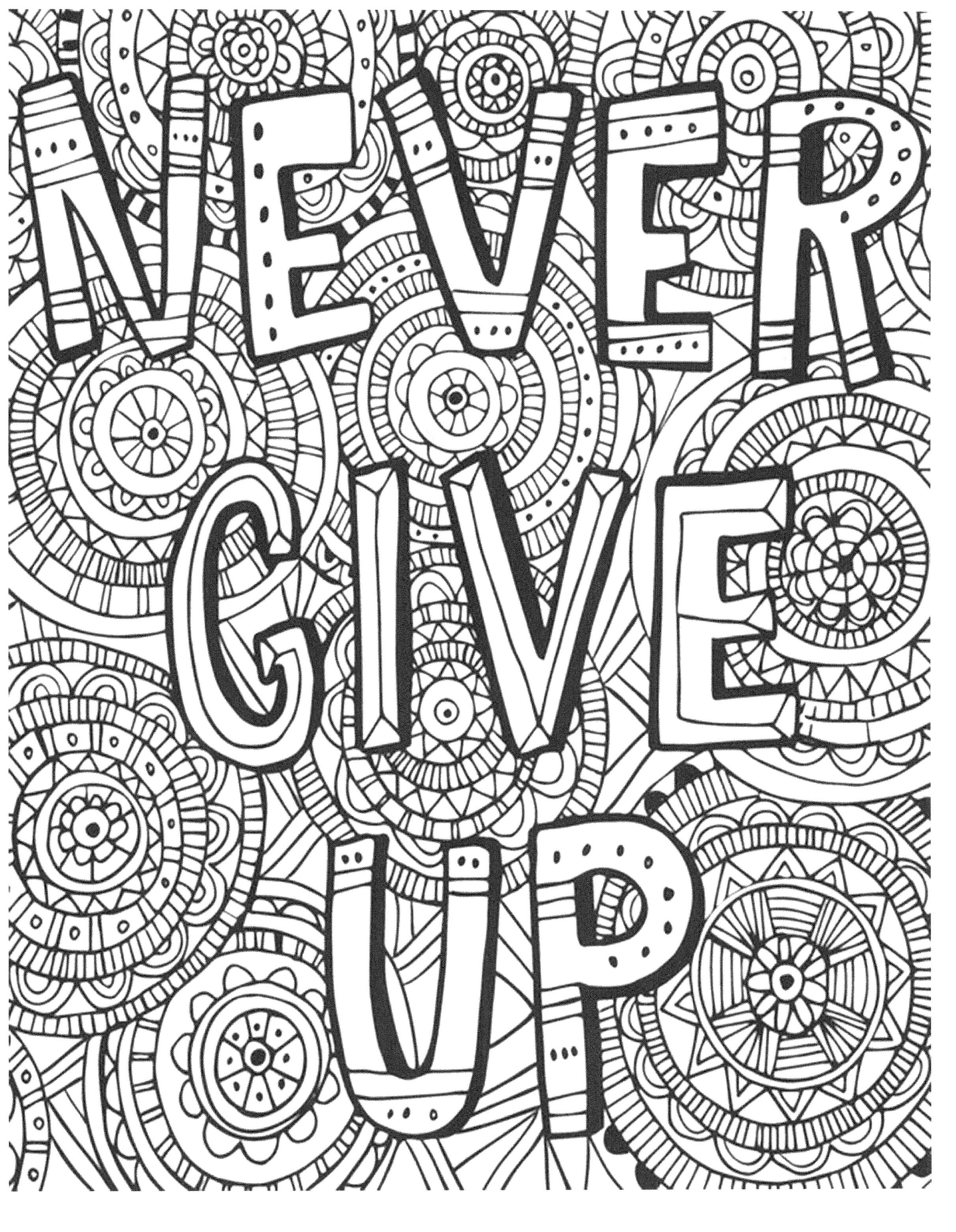

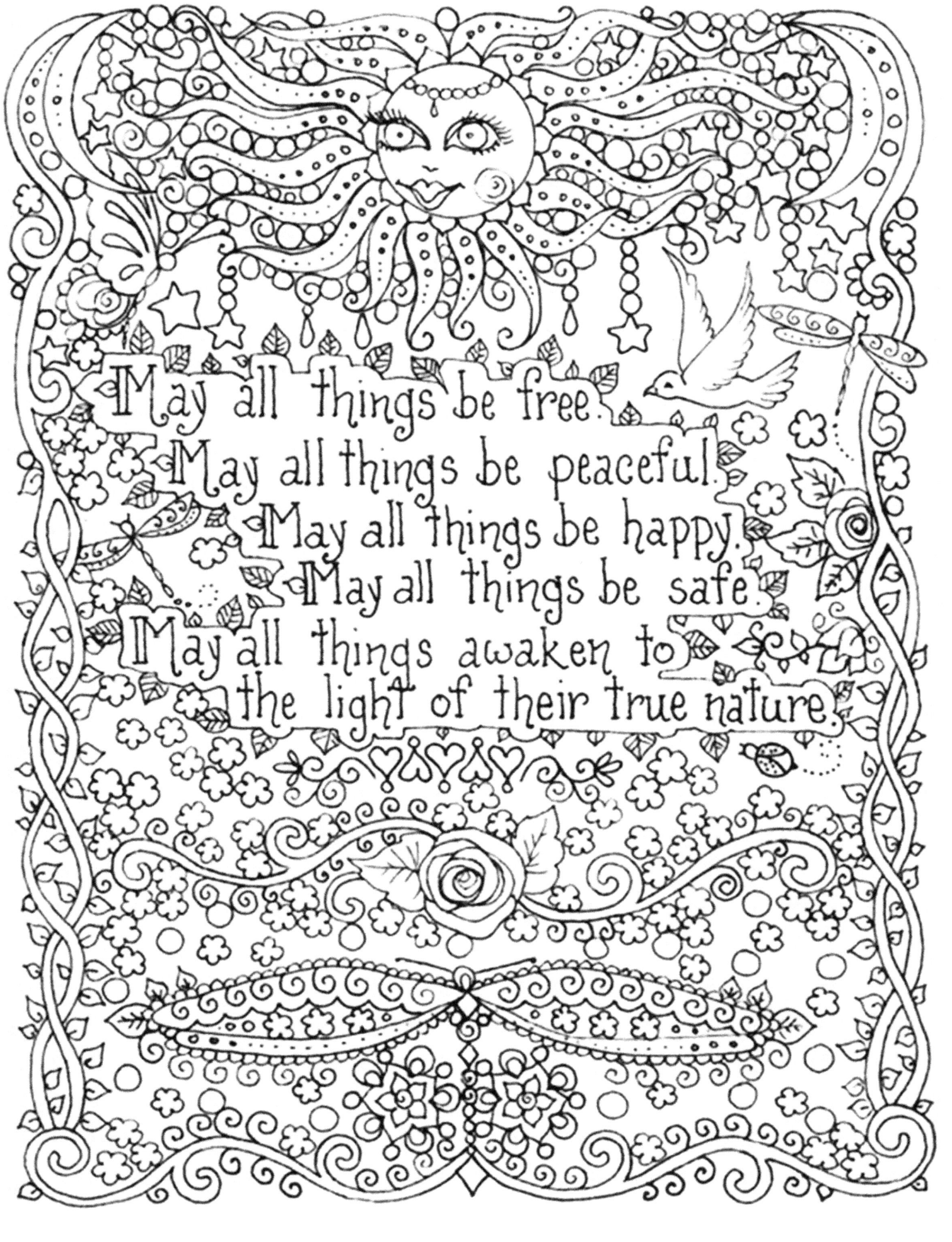

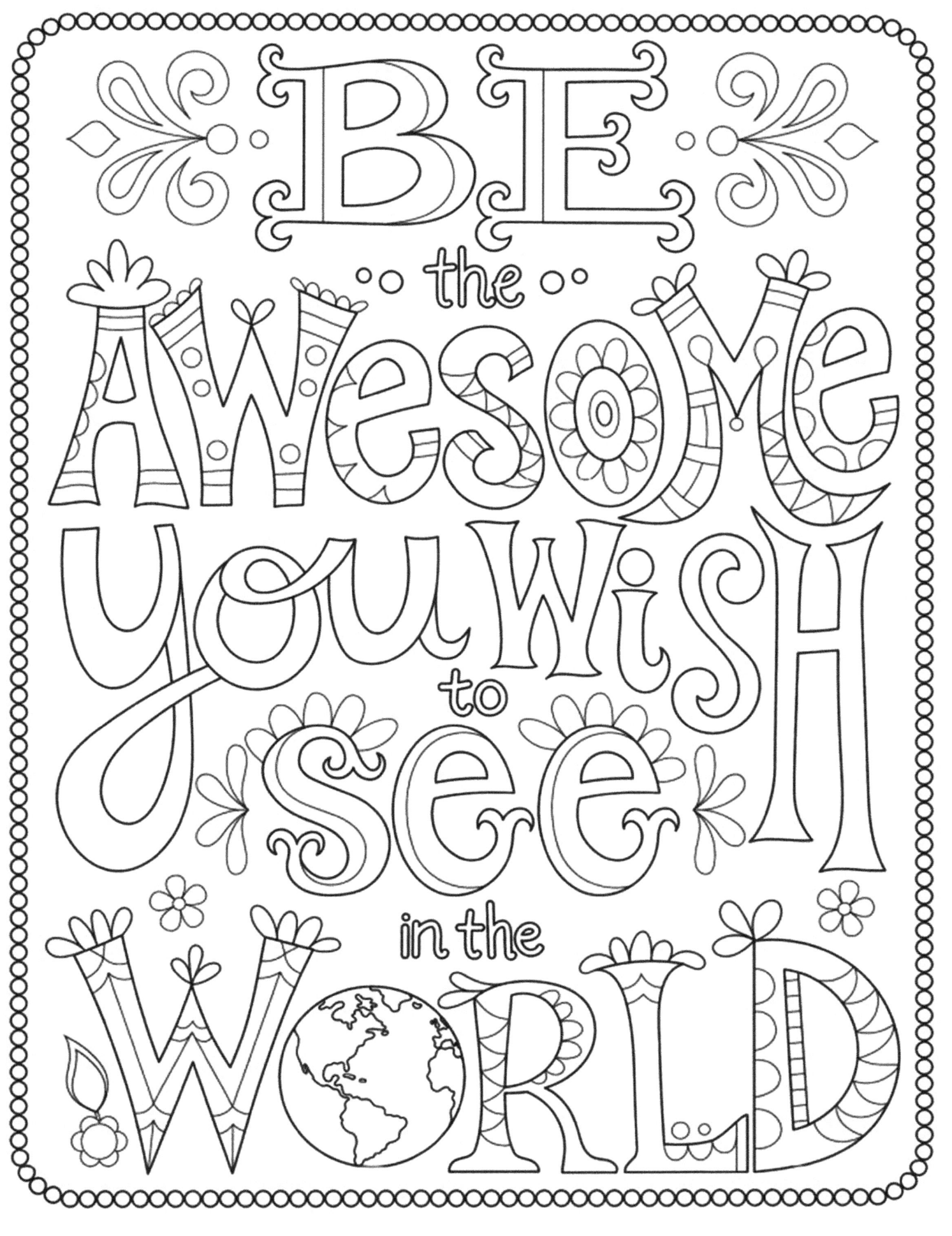

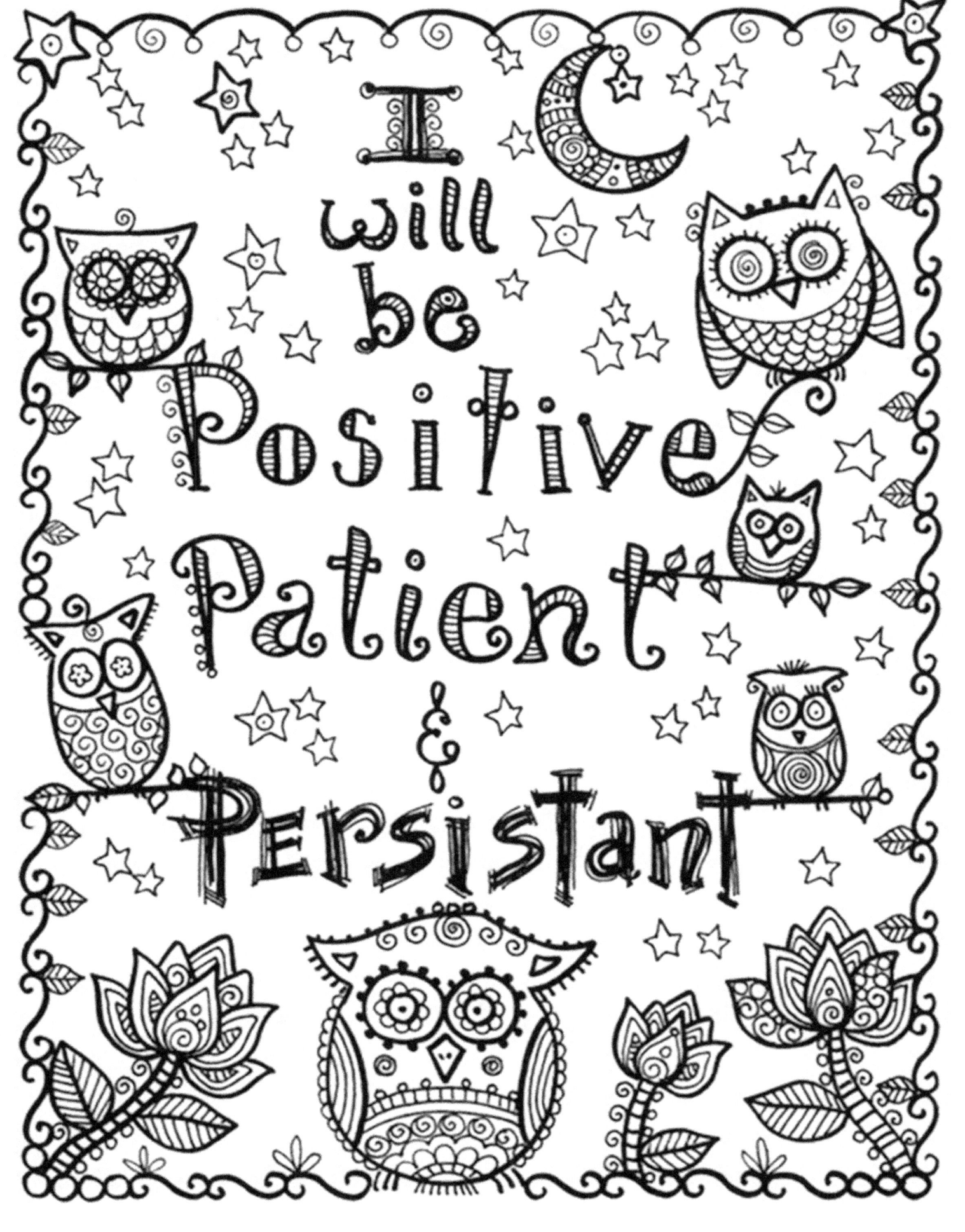

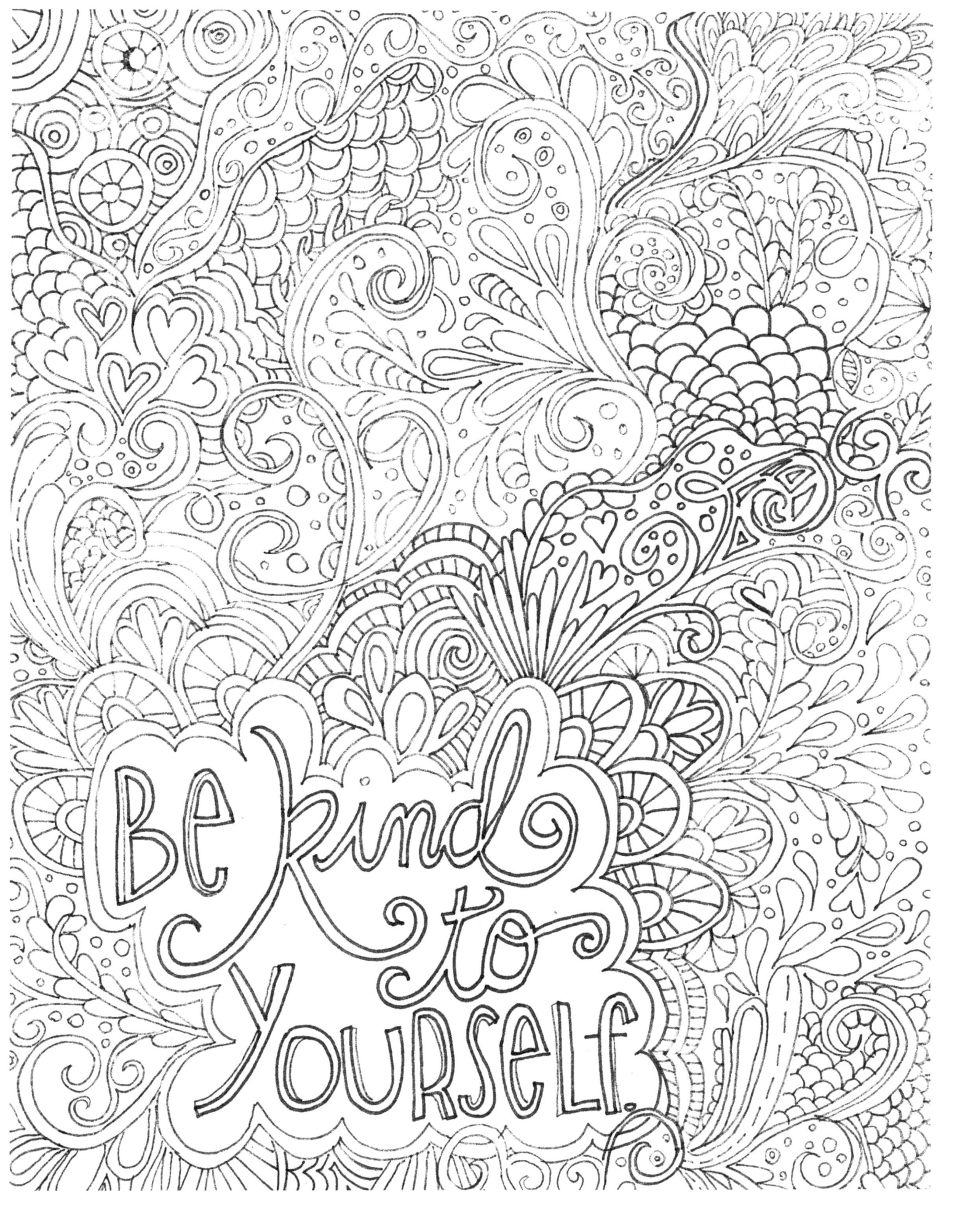

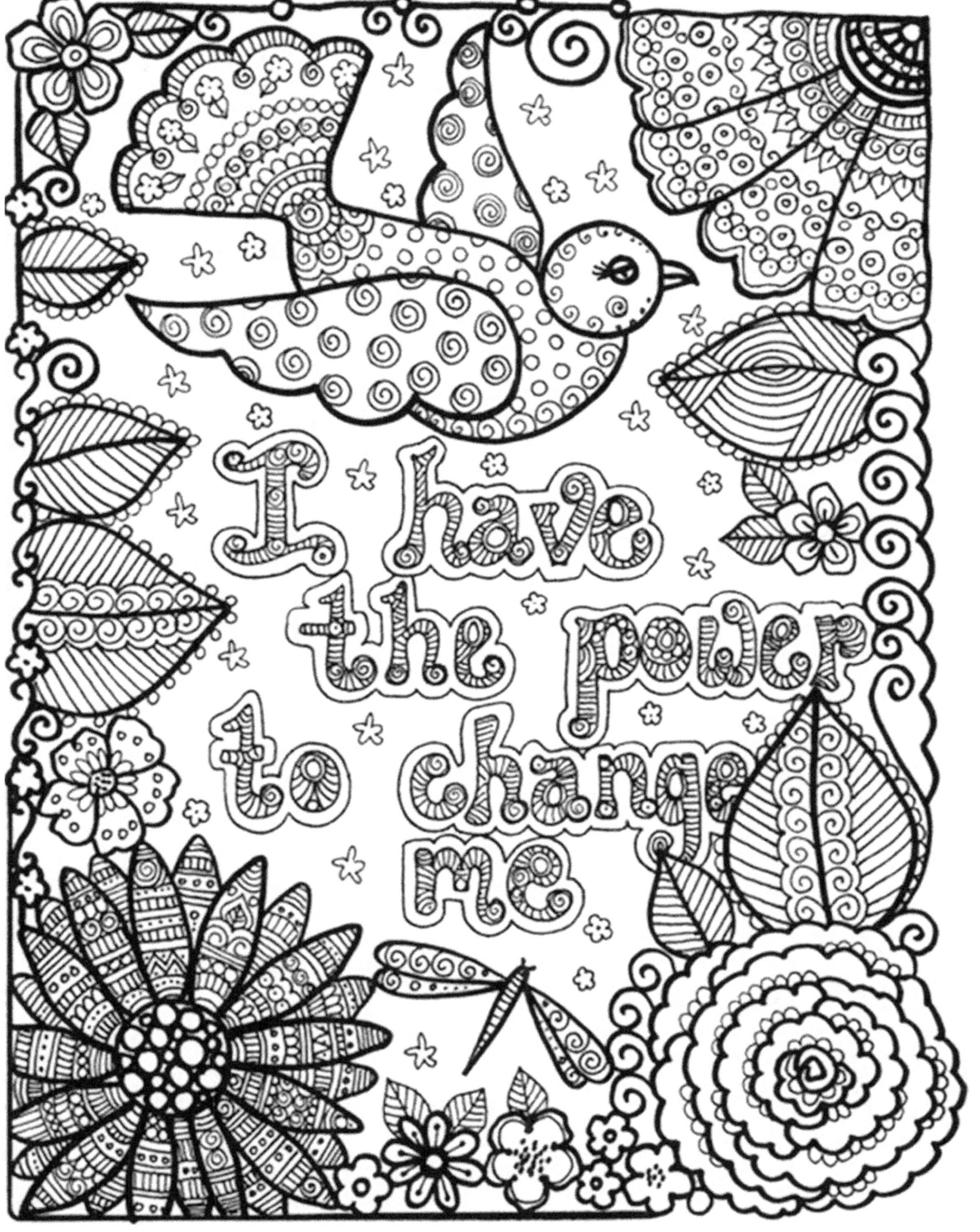

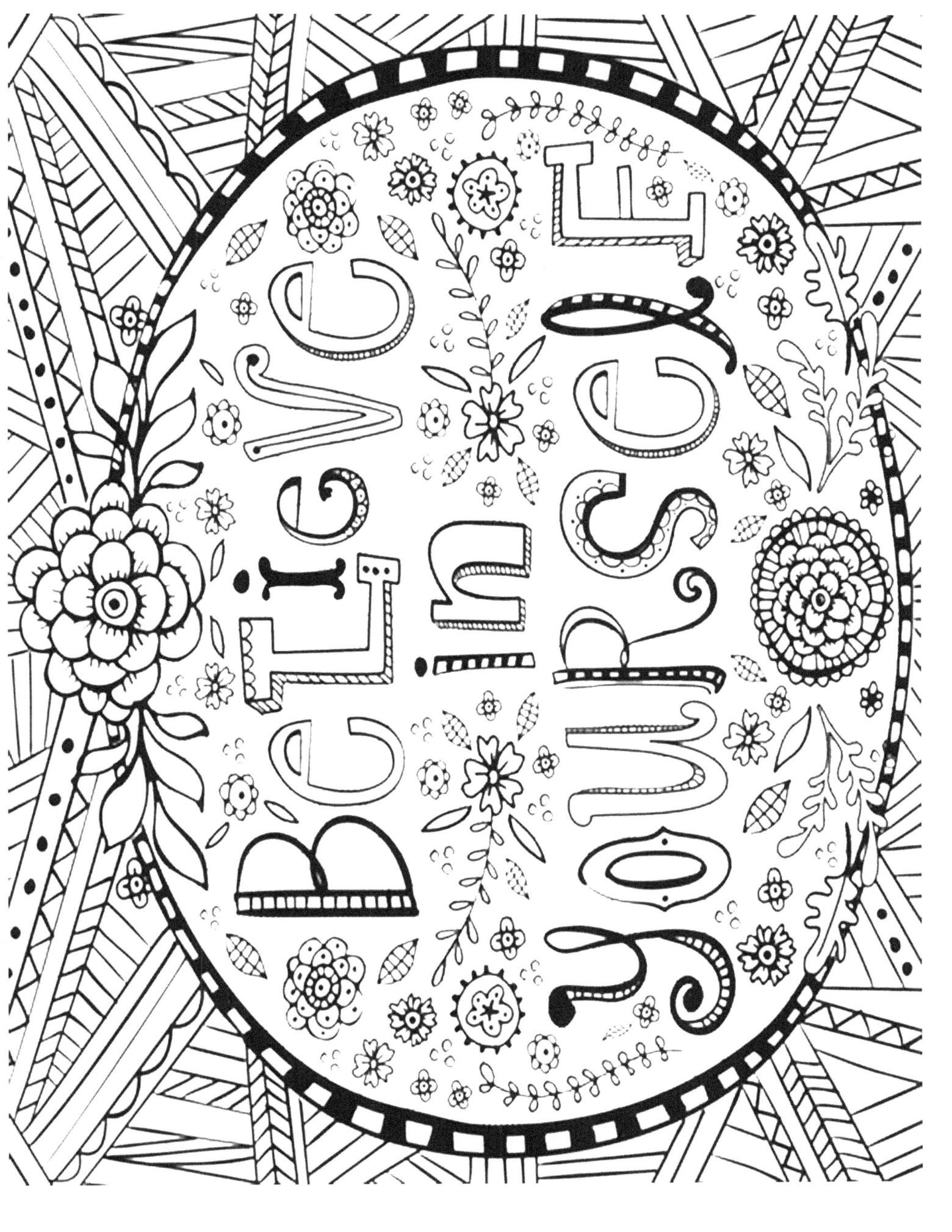

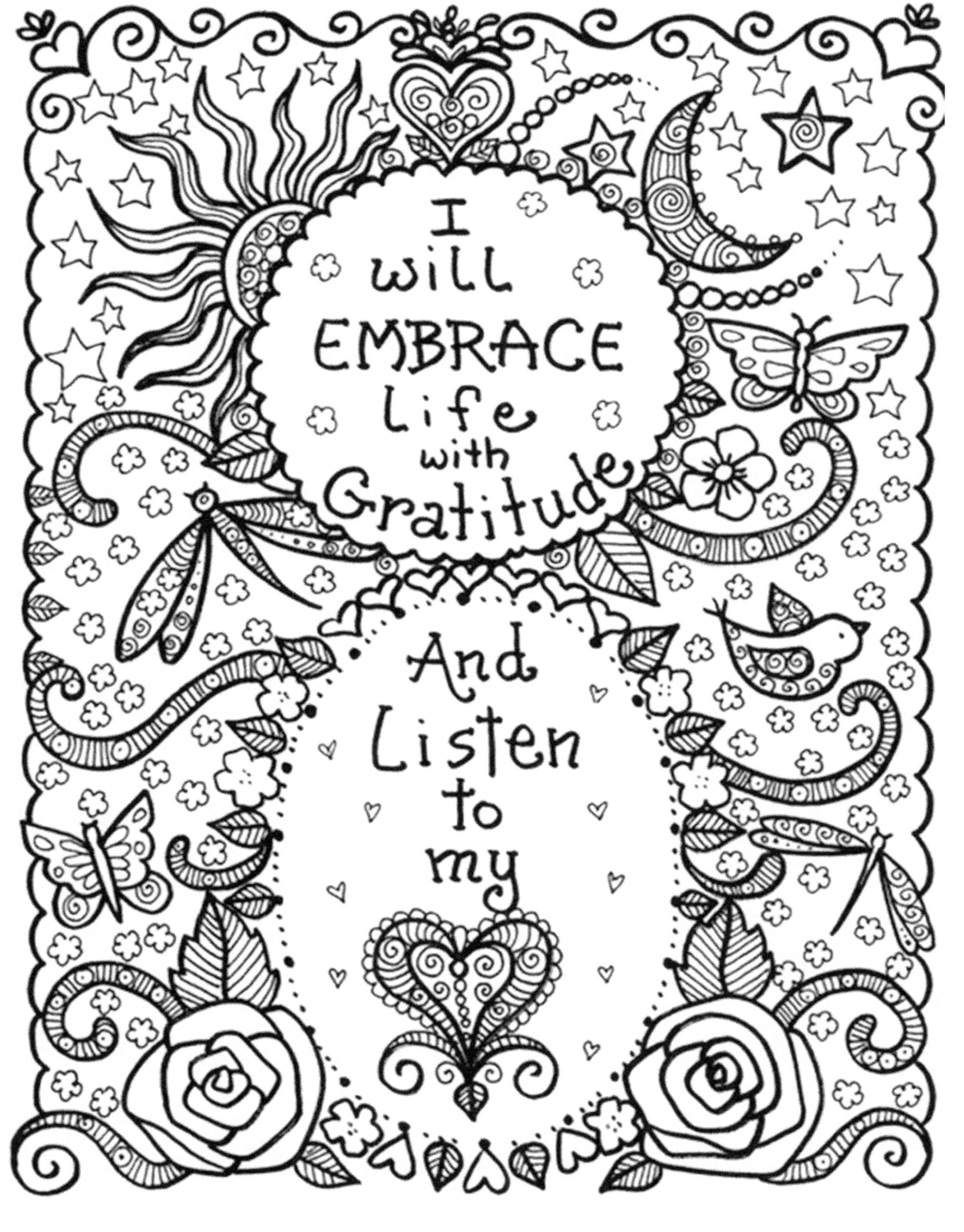

I will EMBRACE life with Gratitude

And Listen to my

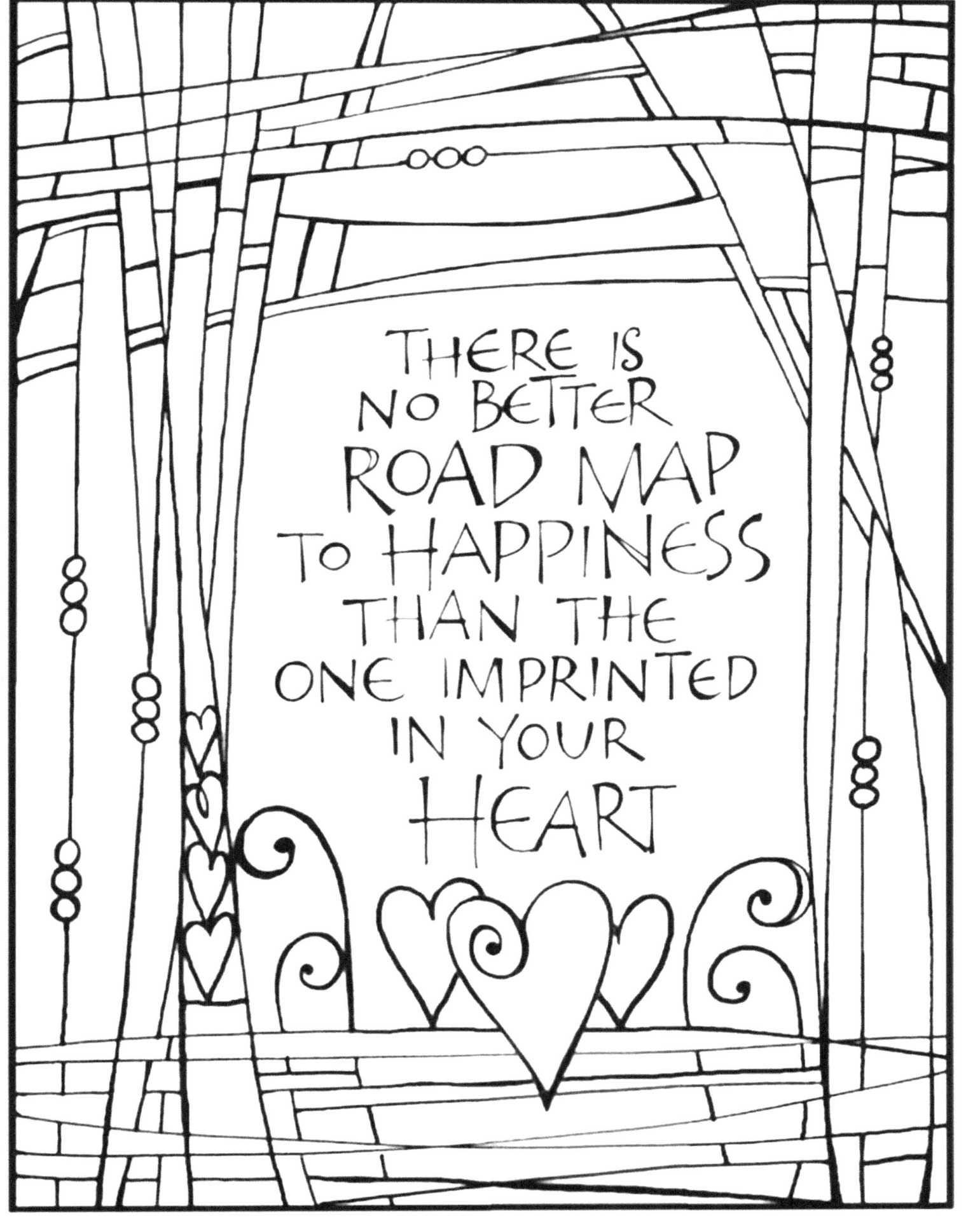

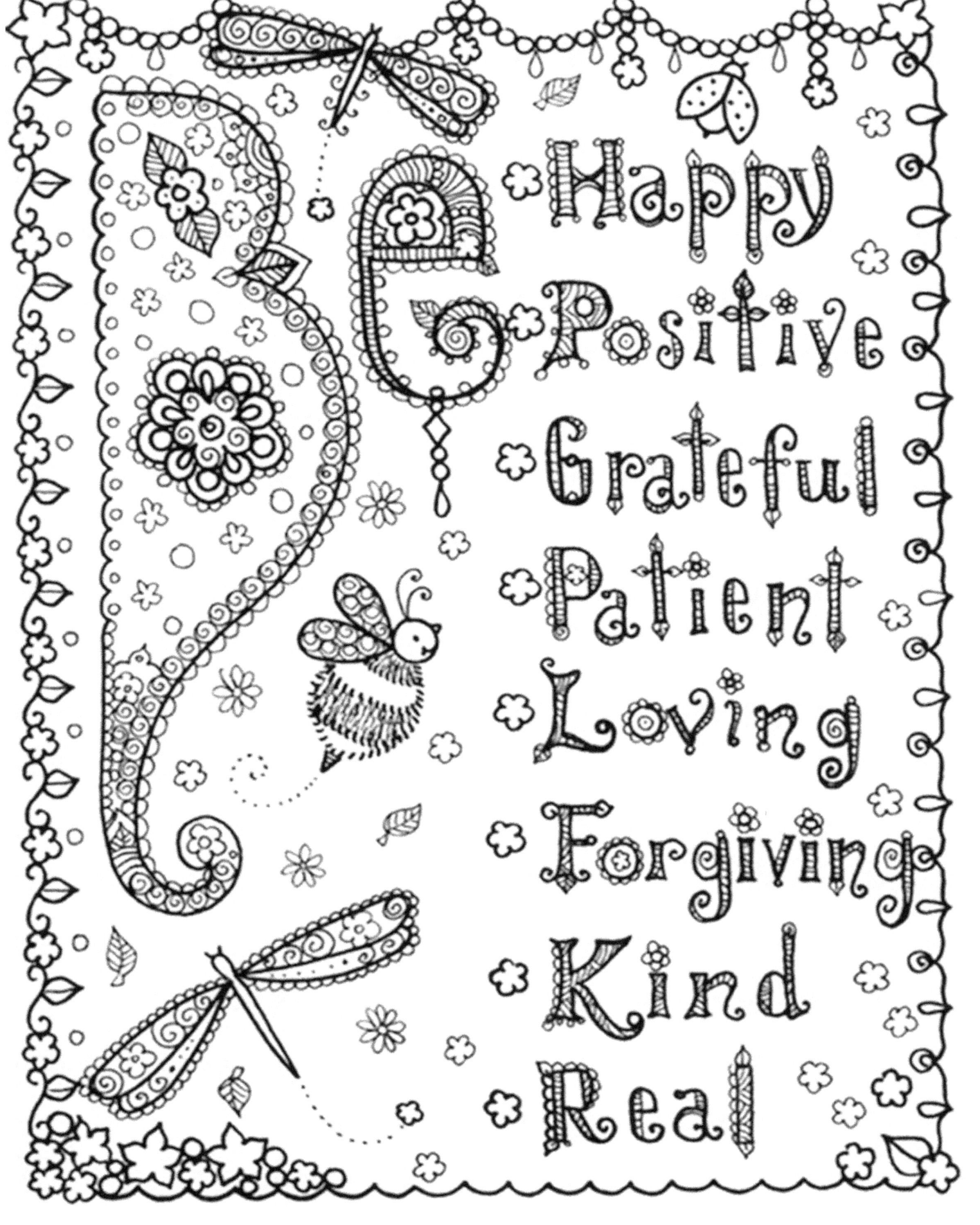

Be

Happy
Positive
Grateful
Patient
Loving
Forgiving
Kind
Real

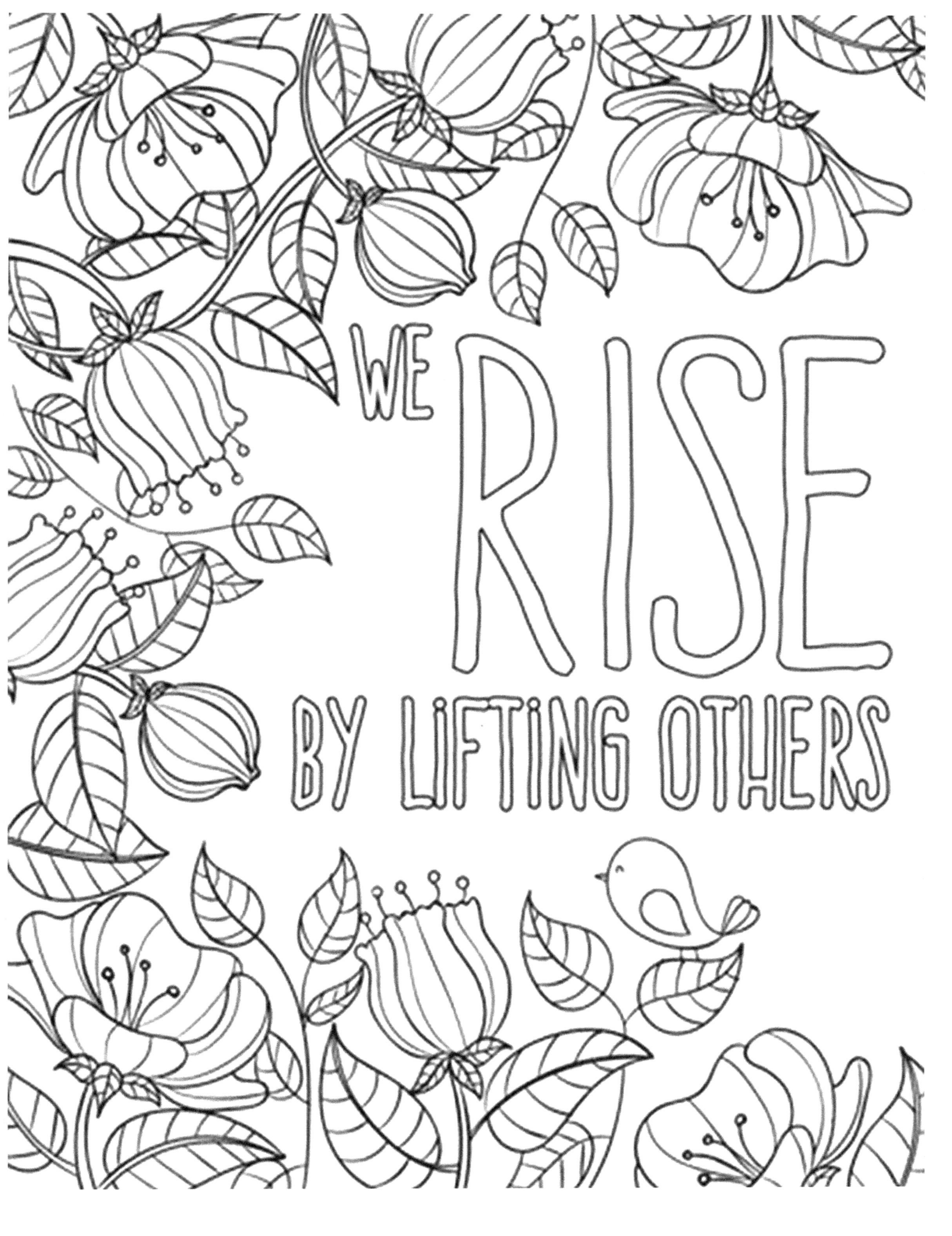

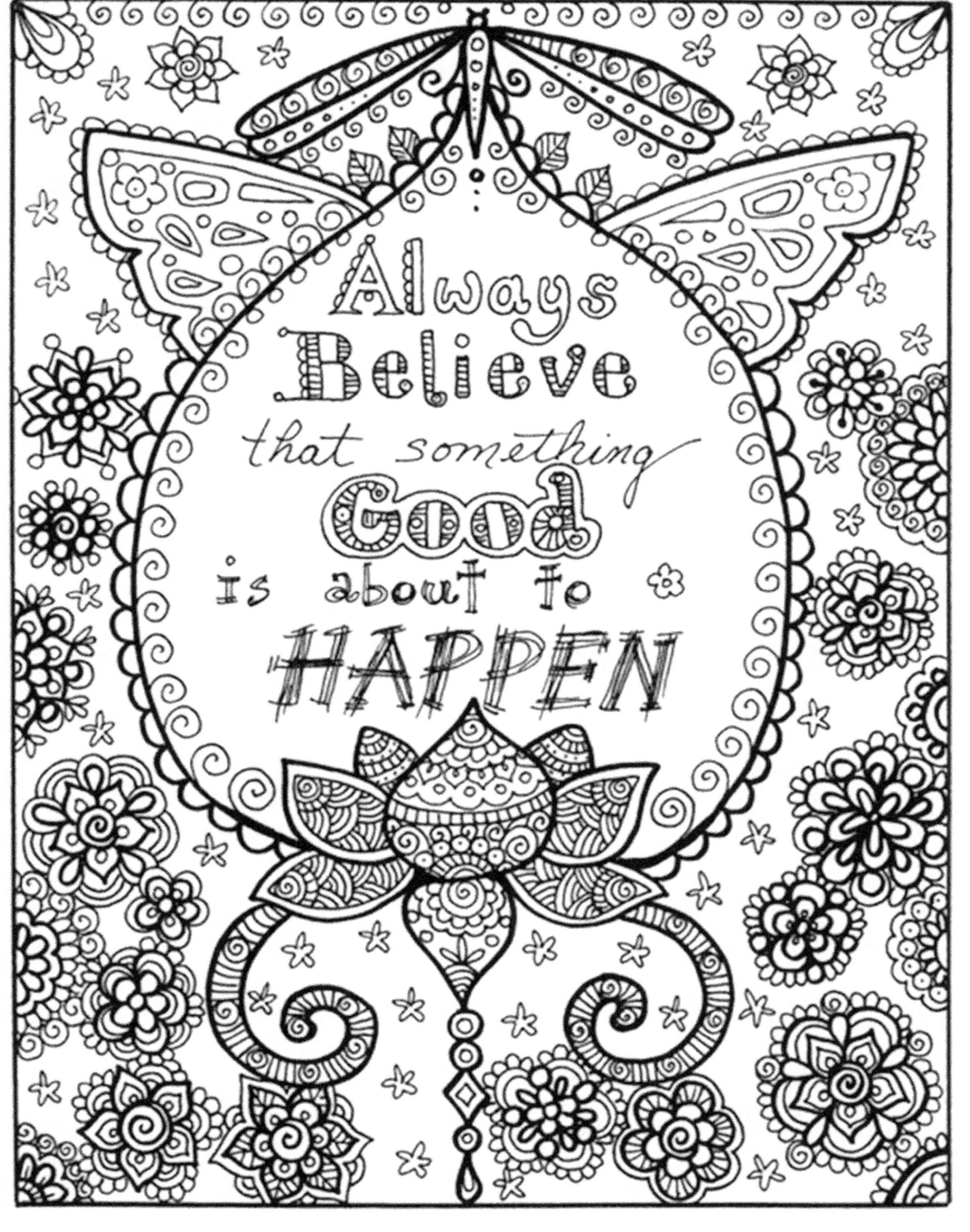

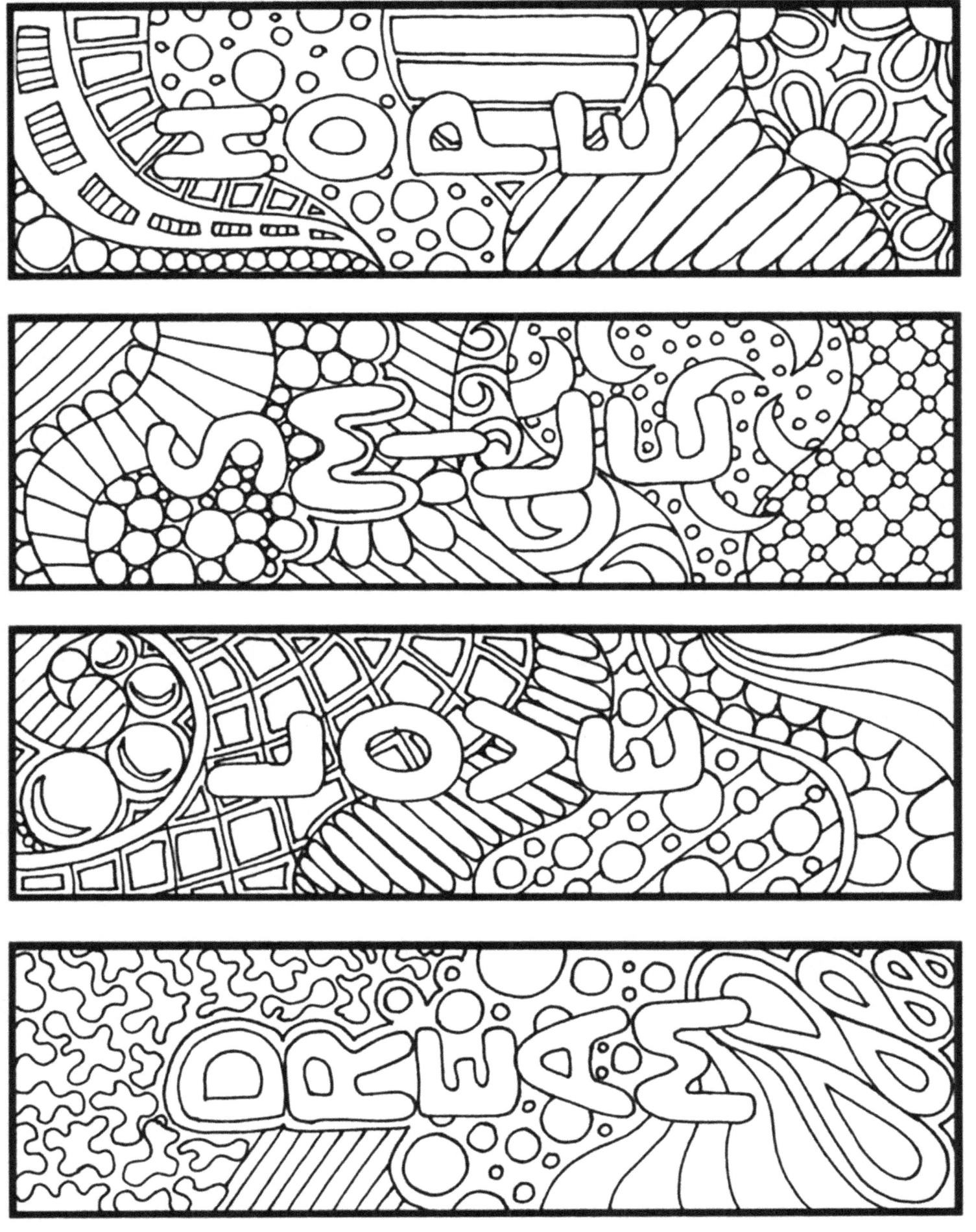

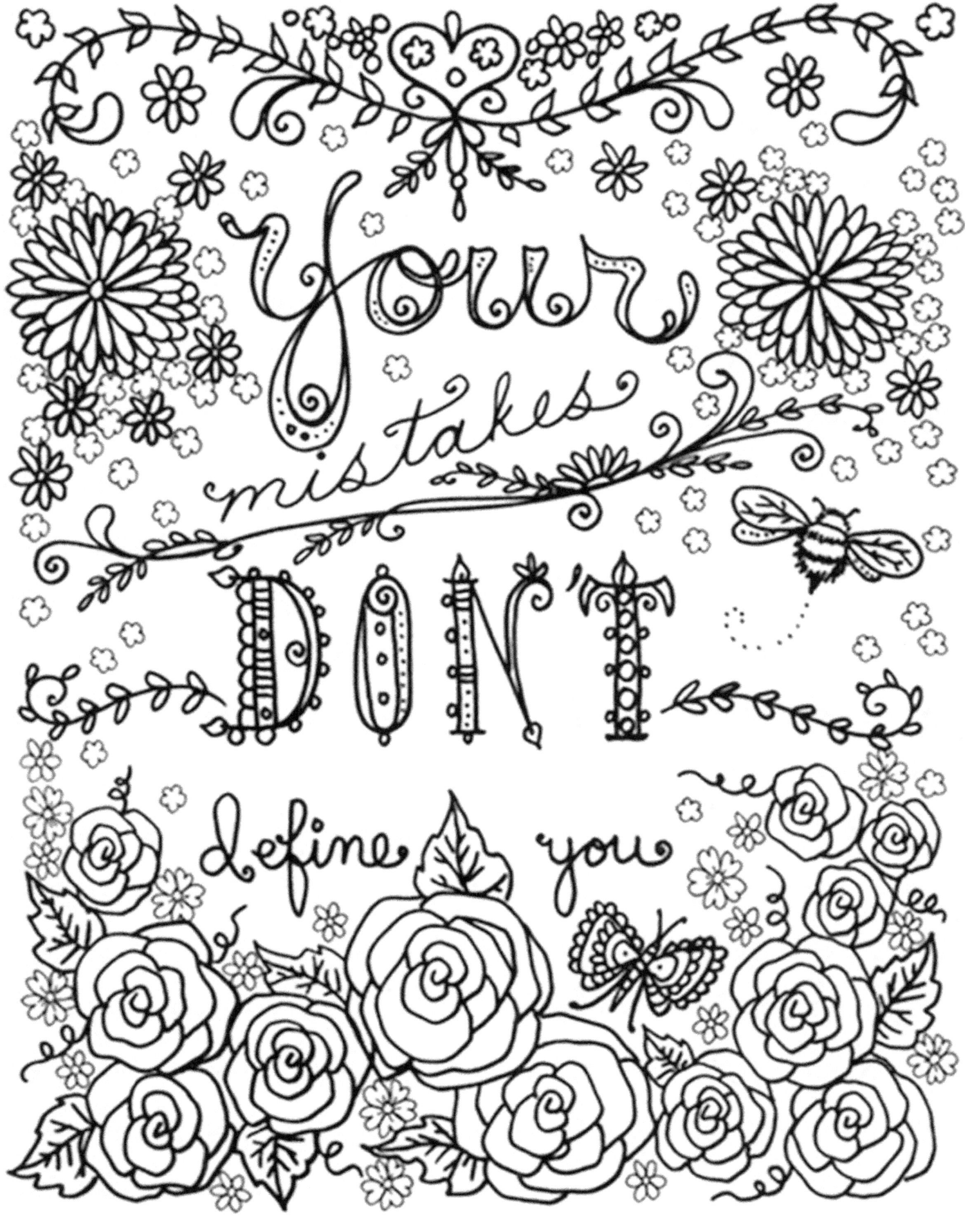

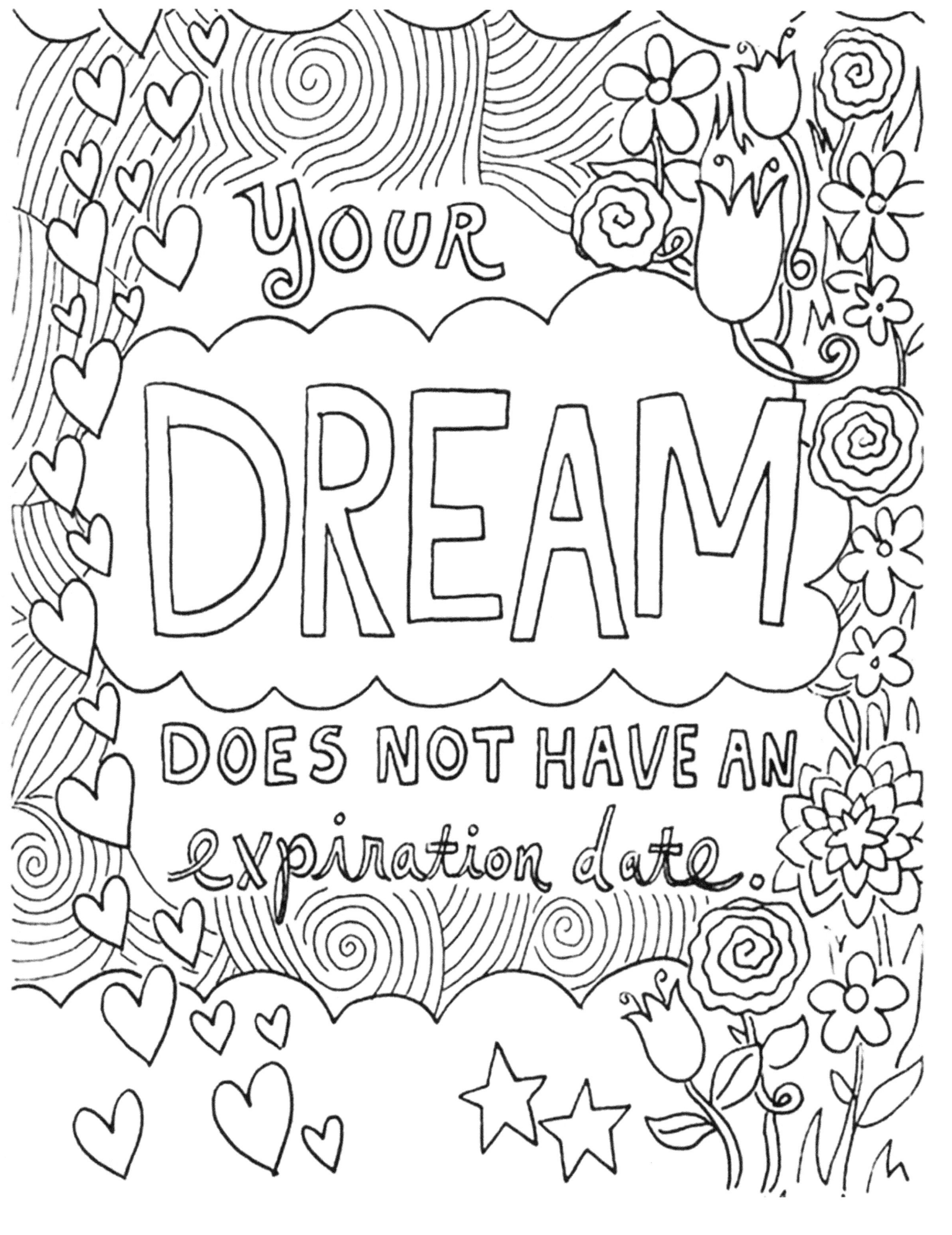

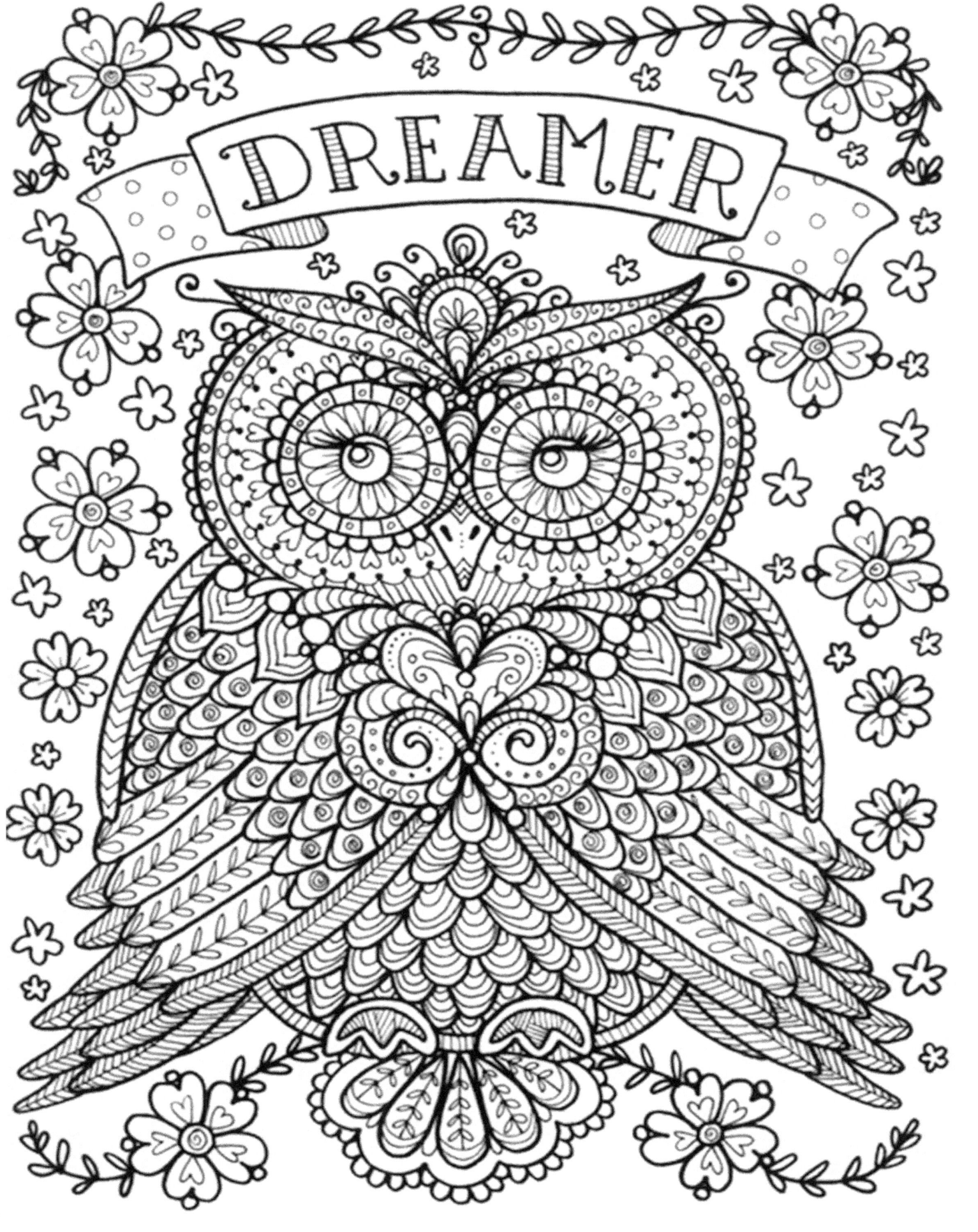

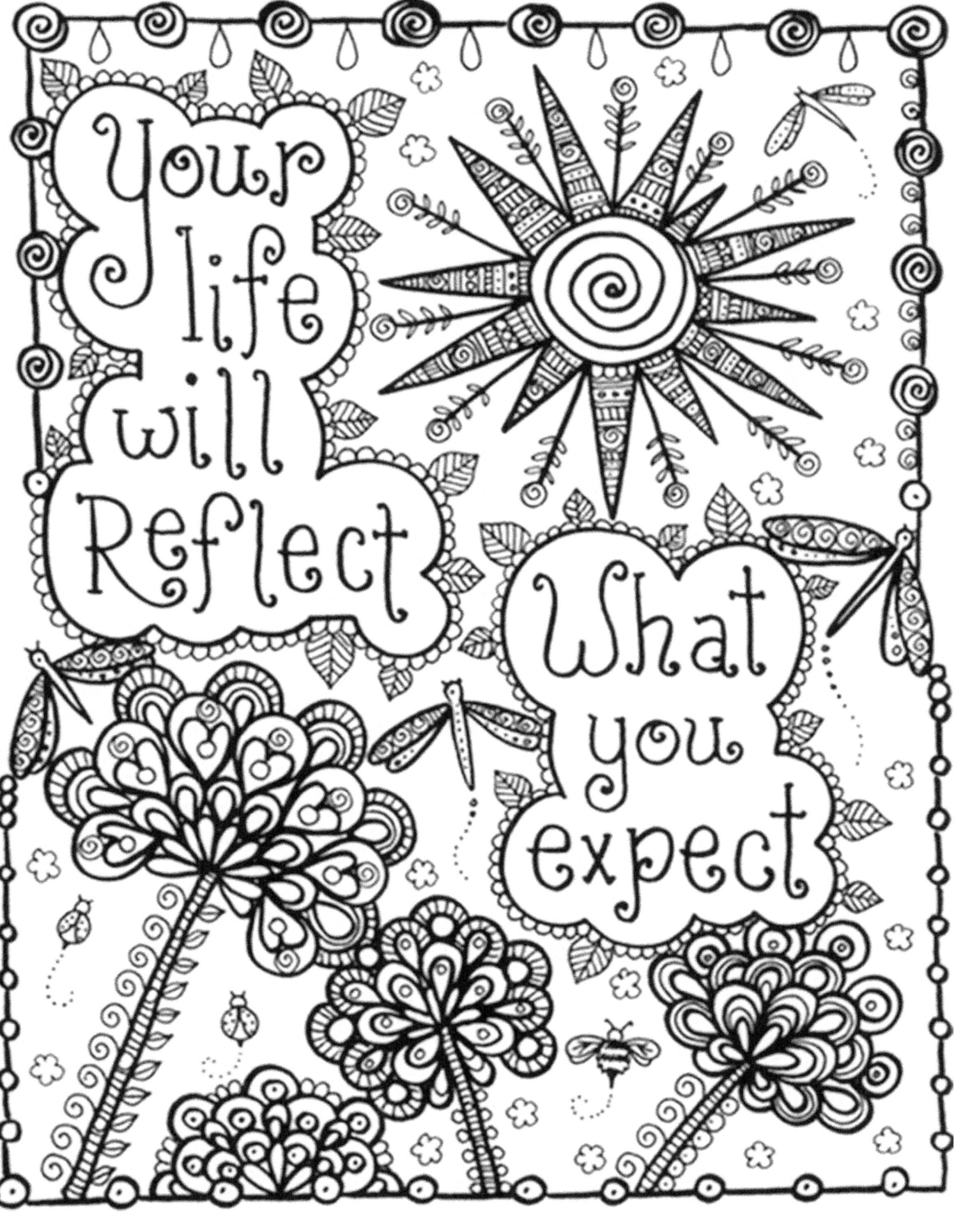

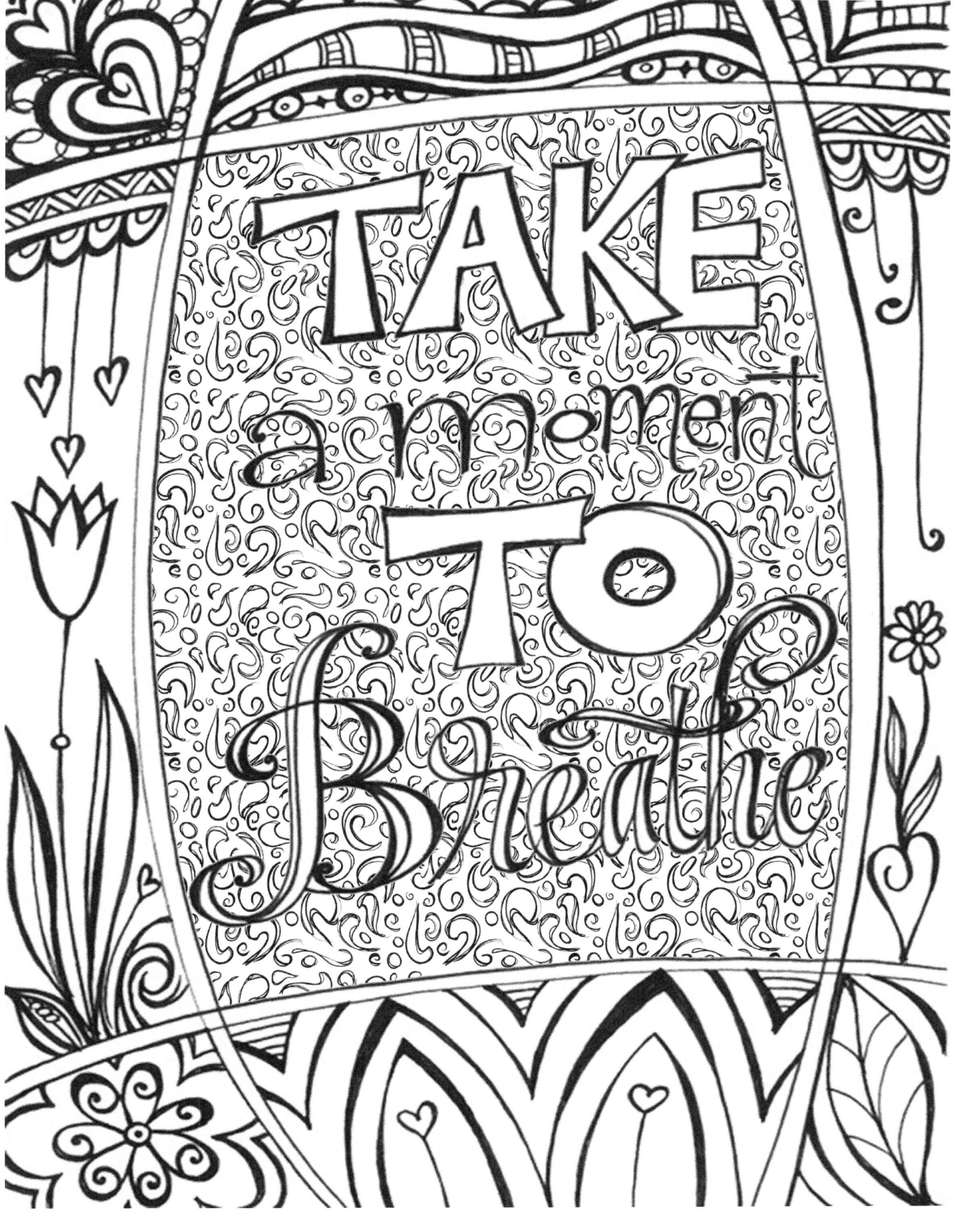

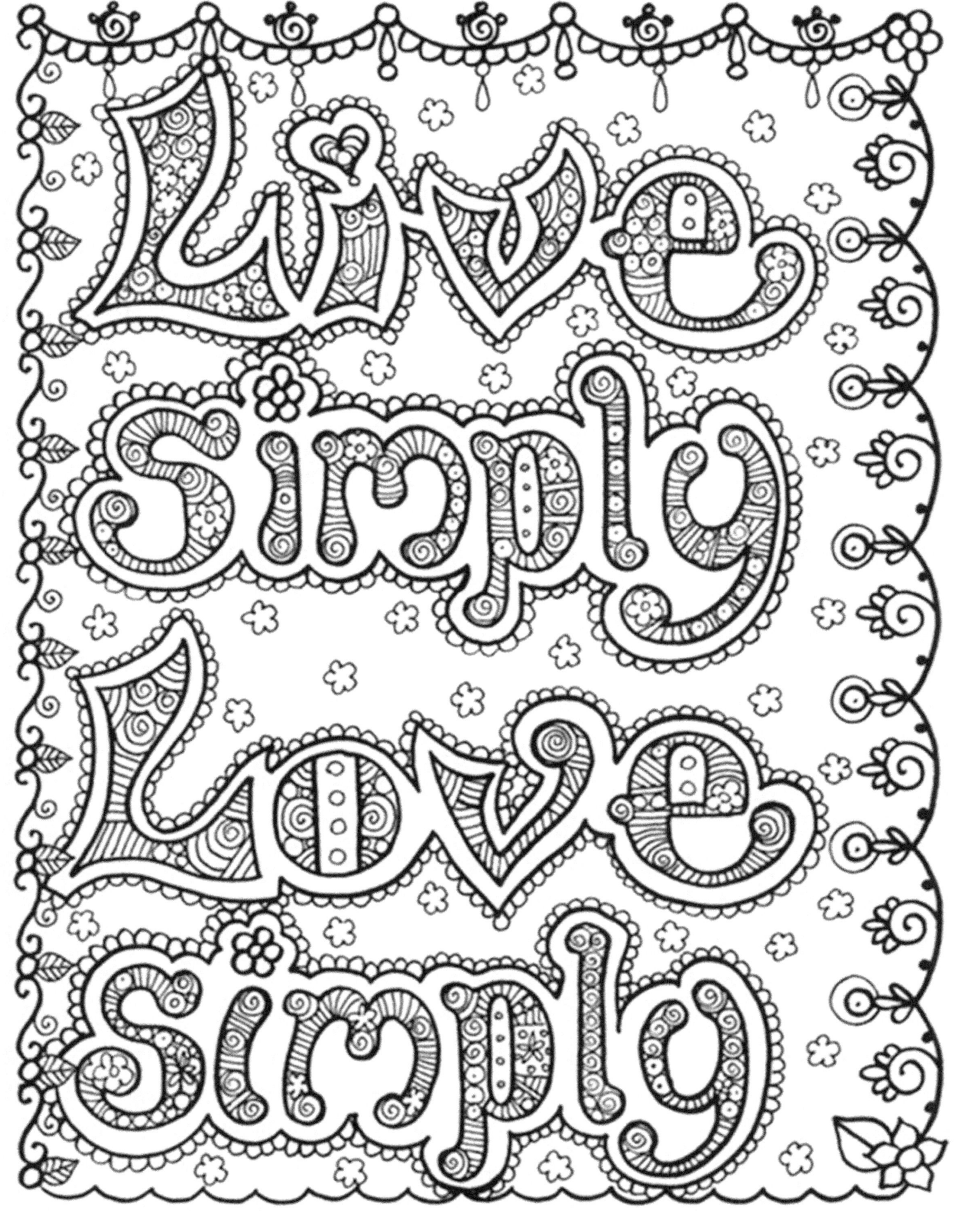

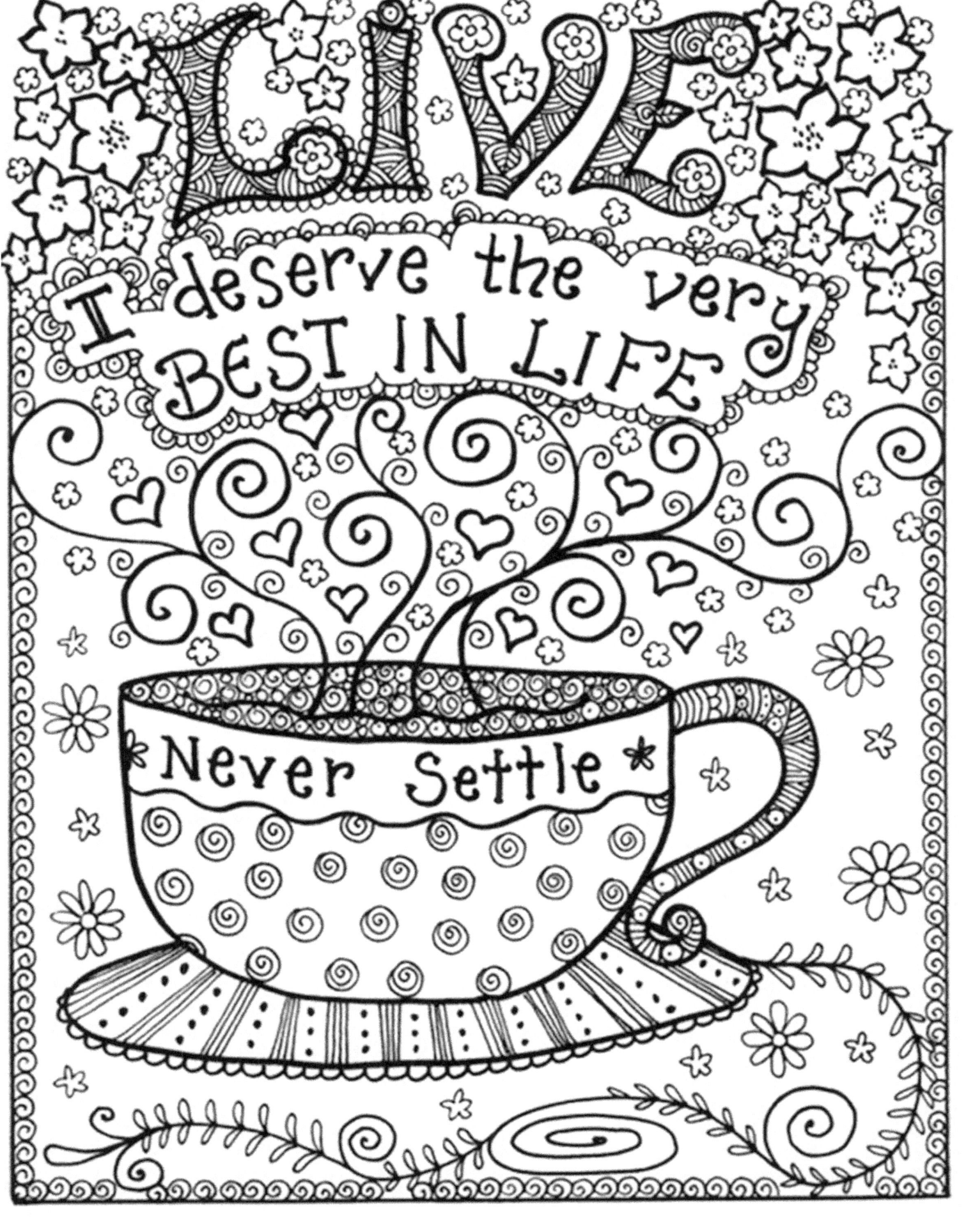

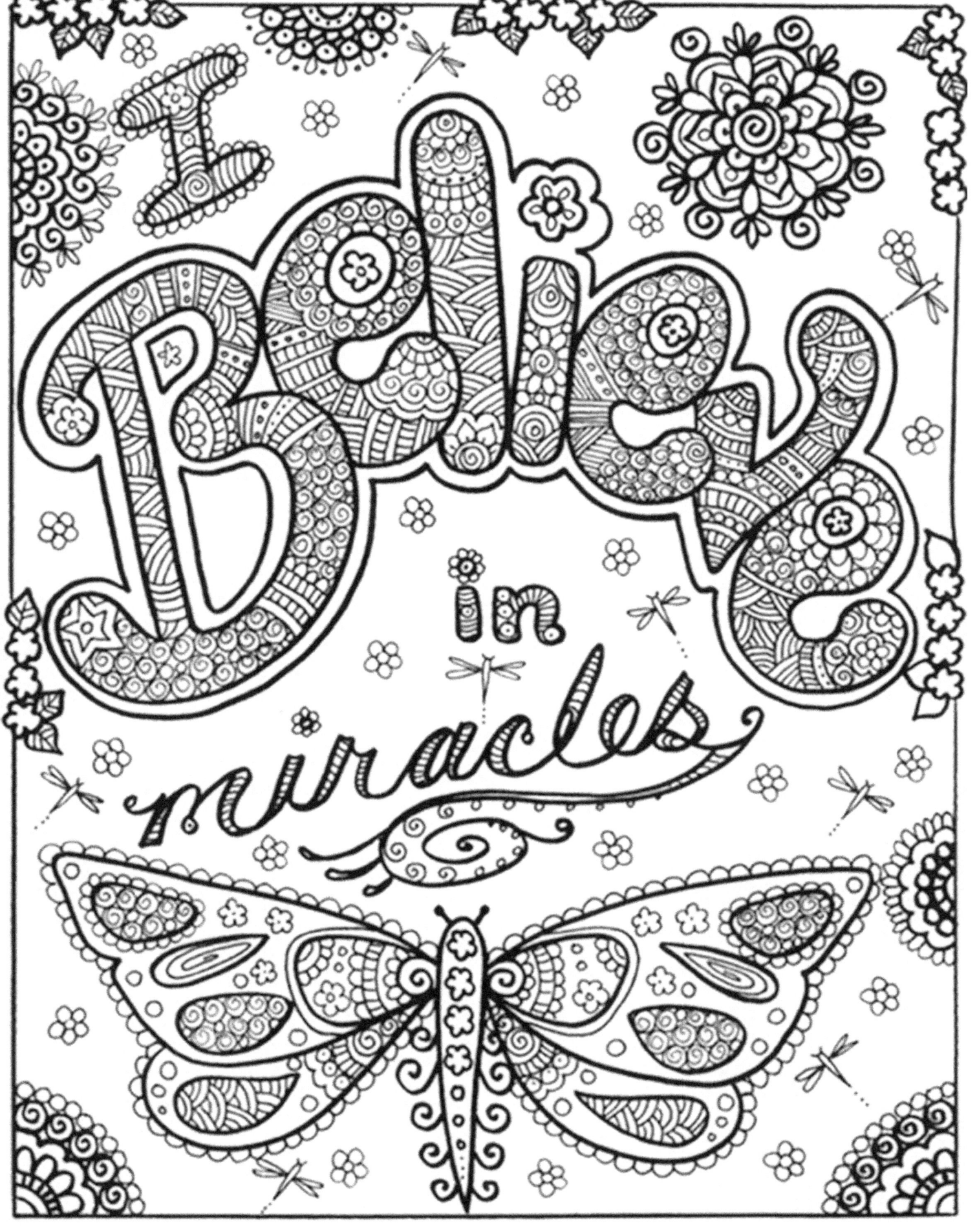

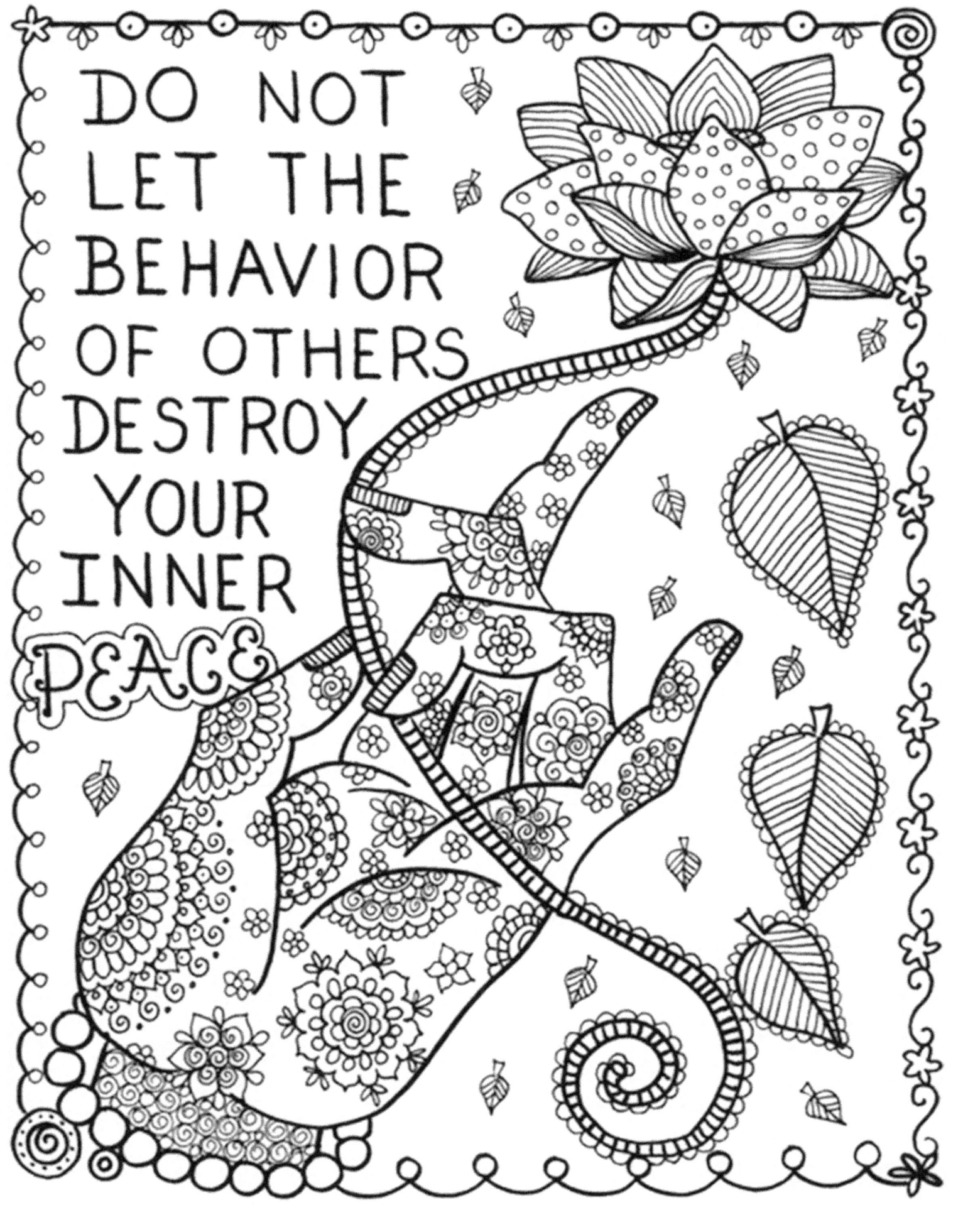

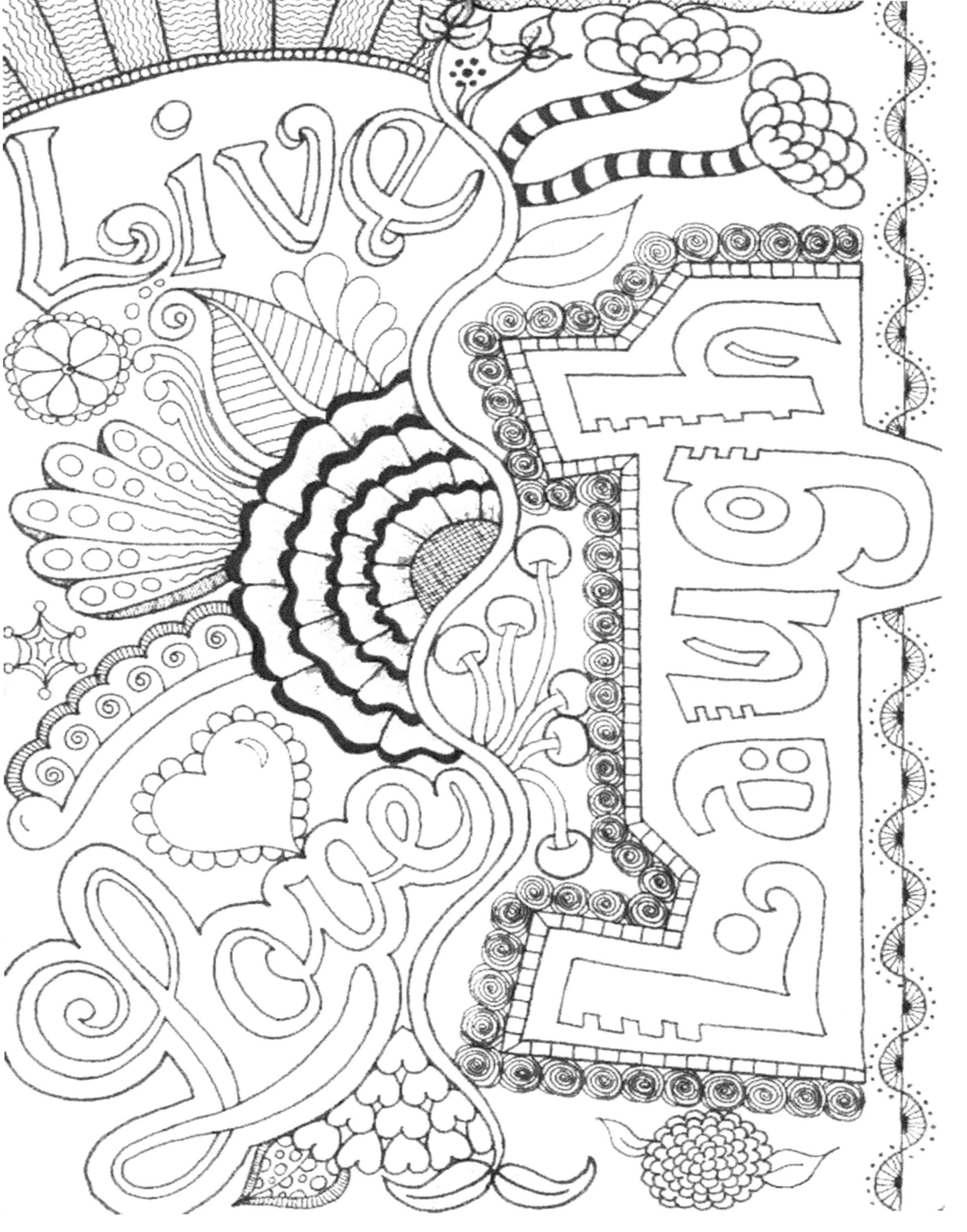

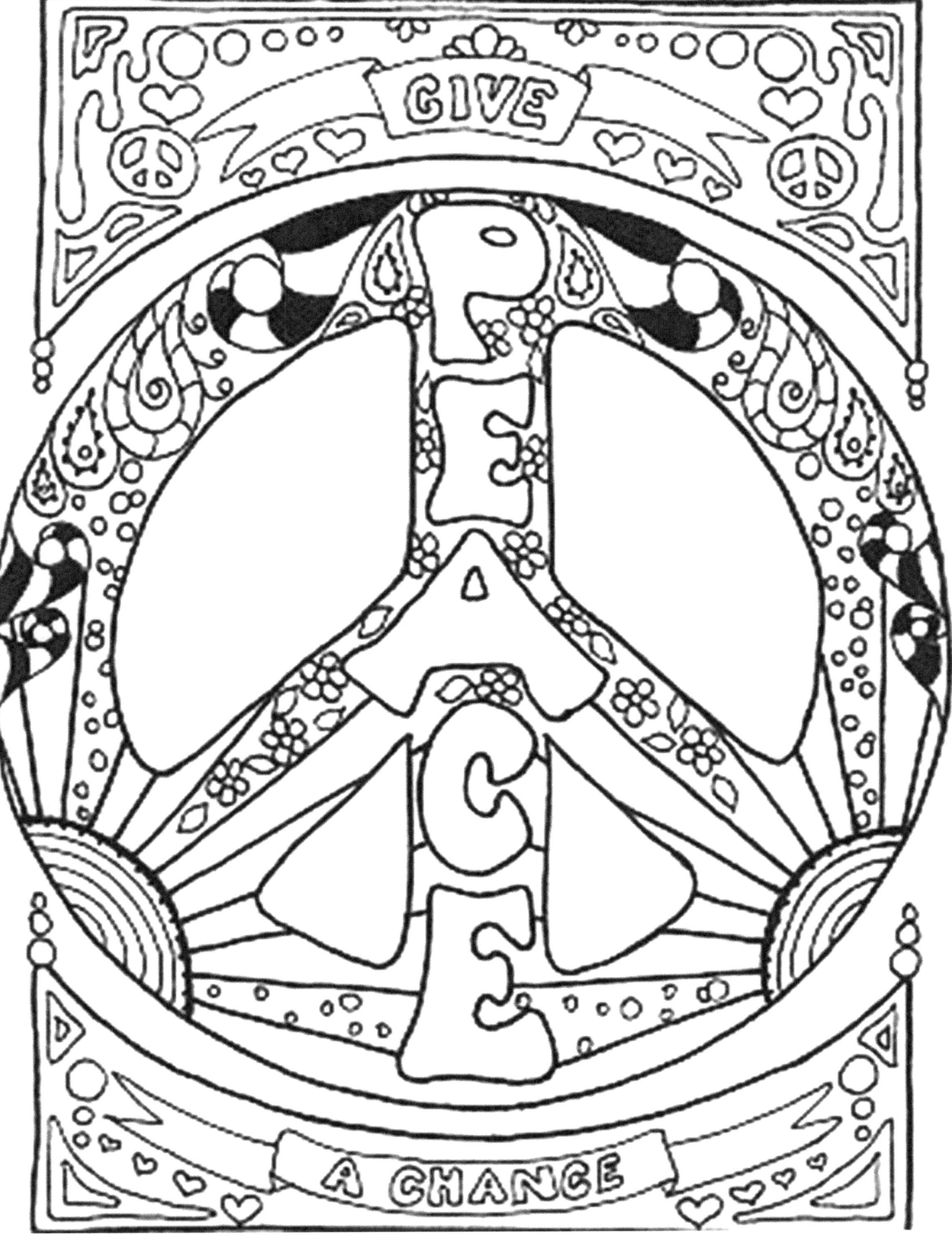

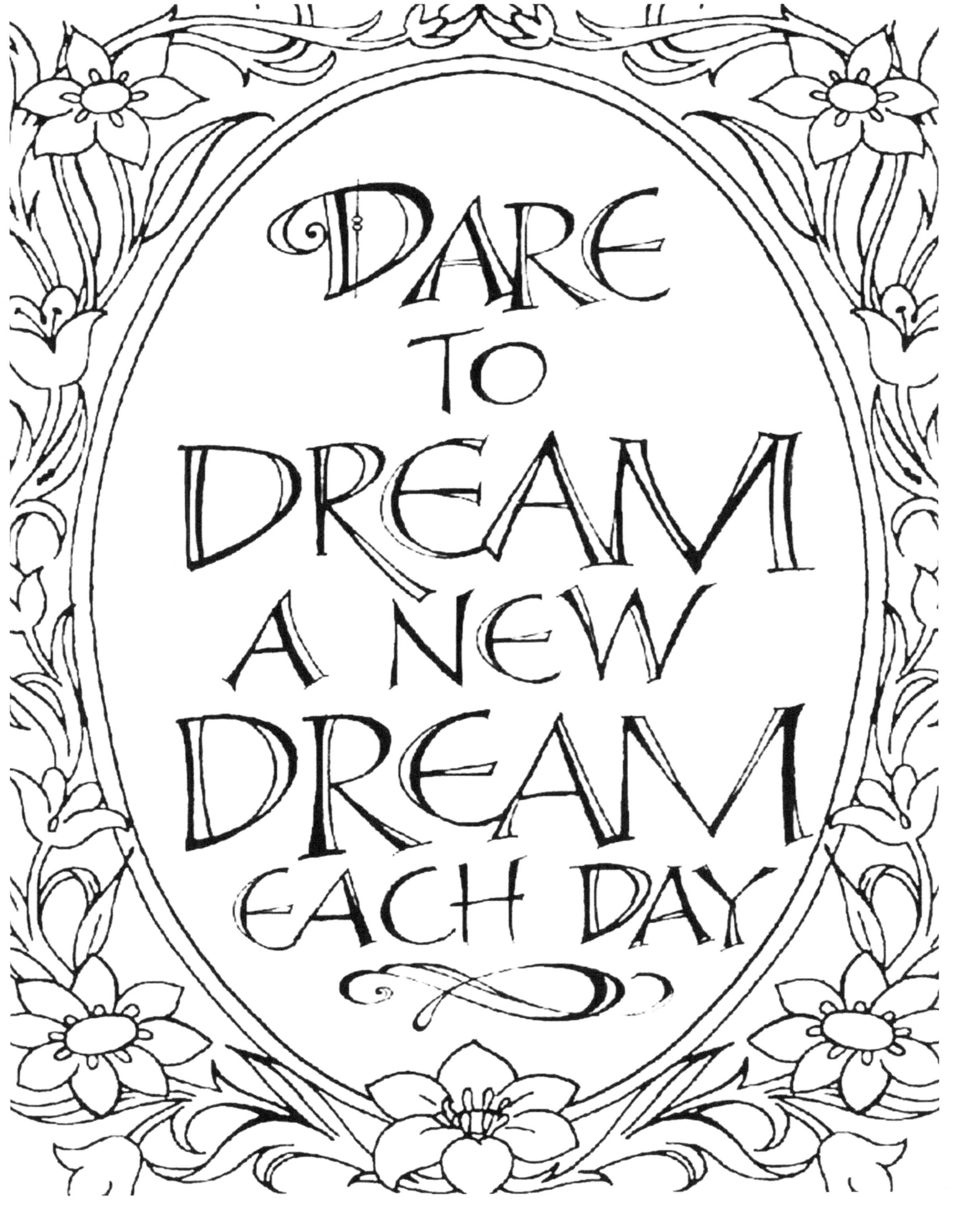

www.ingramcontent.com/pod-product-compliance
Lightning Source LLC
Chambersburg PA
CBHW080540190526

45169CB00007B/2580